HOMAGE TO EUGENE O'NEILL

Literary Criticism in a New Key

Bruce Fleming

University Press of America,® Inc.
Lanham · Boulder · New York · Toronto · Plymouth, UK

Copyright © 2008 by
Bruce Fleming
4501 Forbes Boulevard
Suite 200
Lanham, Maryland 20706
UPA Acquisitions Department (301) 459-3366

Estover Road
Plymouth PL6 7PY
United Kingdom

All rights reserved
Printed in the United States of America
British Library Cataloging in Publication Information Available

Library of Congress Control Number: 2008920221
ISBN-13: 978-0-7618-4021-3 (paperback : alk. paper)
ISBN-10: 0-7618-4021-4 (paperback : alk. paper)

™ The paper used in this publication meets the minimum
requirements of American National Standard for Information
Sciences—Permanence of Paper for Printed Library Materials,
ANSI Z39.48—1984

Contents

Preface   *v*

Homage to Eugene O'Neill   *1*

Notes   *97*

Bibilography   *99*

Index   *101*

About the Author   *103*

PREFACE

In *Philosophy in a New Key* (1957), Suzanne K. Langer proposed that it was time for philosophy and literary criticism to change their key, in the musical sense—and that to a degree, this switch in musical key had already begun. The particular key she thought the tonality of the future was defined by symbolic and ritualistic thought. As things turned out, while this sort of approach to the arts had its brief period of prominence, it soon faded out. Thus Langer may in retrospect seem to have beat the drum too loudly for a particular way of thought that interested her. Yet if Langer was wrong in the particular, it seems she was right in the general. The emphasis on ritual and symbolic thought she was concerned with was certainly an early example of the way that literary criticism came to be done in the second half of the twentieth century, with reactions to literature substituting for the artwork itself as the center of academic attention. This is now the "old" key to which a yet newer one is, I believe, in the process of succeeding—and in any case, should succeed.

This book, whose sub-title is "Literary Criticism in a New Key," suggests it's time for the key in which we play the relation between criticism and artwork to change again, this time to a key that has largely gone unheard since before the cultural cataclysm of Romanticism. We should be clear that if the key changes, the kind of product we produce changes as well. Indeed, it may no longer be possible to speak of "literary criticism" after the change in key: we may in fact cease producing a certain kind of product and begin producing another. The new kind is exemplified by the present work.

Slice of the pie

Artwork and critical reaction vie for the same slice of the pie, the reader's time and attention. Any given hour can be spent on reading a poem/novel/play, or on reading criticism about any of these, or a combination of artwork and criticism, where maximizing one means minimizing the other. Different eras have offered different combinations of these two elements, with criticism and critical reaction assuming the various forms they did depending on the way the artwork, to which criticism is related, is itself conceived.

The disappearance of one sort of written product and the appearance, or re-appearance, of another is in itself no cause for regret, except from those who are attached to or invested in the old way of doing things. People constantly find new things to do; only those who cannot conceive of anything but what they grew up with will find this threatening. This is true of reactions to artworks and also of artworks themselves: artistic forms aren't eternal, though they may seem so to their practitioners at the time.

The realistic novel, to take an obvious example, developed in post-Renaissance, neo-classical England, taking as its prototype works from earlier traditions. Other standard examples of correlation of forms to times include the fact that the Medieval Age was a time devoid of secular drama; overt portraiture of individuals only came into its own with the Renaissance, and so on. In the same way, the West has not always produced "literary criticism" as we think of it today; it stands to reason that the time may come when we no longer think it necessary. I suggest that this time is fast approaching; indeed it may already be here: literary criticism as a separate undertaking from literature has played itself out. This in turn suggests a form of literary criticism, if we wish to call it that, that's not a separate undertaking from literature.

Romantic creation

In the half-century that followed Langer's book, the enterprise of literary consideration professionalized from verbal consideration of a common text into an enterprise where the reaction gradually took on both the status and place of the primary text. What people did in university classrooms changed character too as a result. Teachers weren't expected merely to preside verbally over a discussion of the literature for the time allotted, but also to write books about literature, and ultimately, teach these instead, or at least the theories contained in them. Literary study became its own end as literary studies, in the years following Langer's book, codified into the proto-scientific teachable methodology of our days, where what we teach and produce is the study rather than the literature, sometimes expressed as a particular angle on literature. The type of product we make as a way to express involvement with the literary work has remained constant for fifty years: it's the dense written-for-specialists presupposes-a-vast-amount-of-previous knowledge quasi-scientific study. Such works have by now taken over the artworks both theoretically and practically: after we're done reading or writing the reactions, who has time for the works?

The dense, written-for-insiders consideration of works that compete for time and energy with the artwork defining literary studies for the last half-century came to be at a certain time in intellectual history as a result of a certain attitude of readers with respect to the work. The existence at all of this sort of work is one expression of the development of the Romantic world-view. Because it came to be, it can cease to be as well. I suggest that it both can and should cease to be, as the circumstances which produced it have altered. The alteration in these circumstances is a result of the fact that professionalized literary studies have become the victim of their own success in professionalizing: the study has taken over the literature. This sort of enterprise serves primarily as the lingua franca of a small priestly caste, and is taught to those who aspire to join that caste. To an increasing degree, others are scared away.

We no longer teach literature to people who don't want to be literature professors, or we teach it as if we think they do, which puzzles and alienates those who stay: we teach the study of literature, not the literature, usually denying that there is such a thing as literature without the study. Even professors, it seems, are tiring of spending so much time reading analysis rather than the literature. Increasingly they are willing to say that they became professors to read novels and poetry: why do they have to read so much writing by professors? Many simply don't. The books keep being produced, but fewer and fewer people read these books: there are just too many of them. No one can "keep up." Library budgets are being slashed, and what remains is devoted to a much larger degree to expensive electronic acquisitions; more is being produced and less bought or read.

New key

It's time for literary criticism in a new key: how can we react to literature in print in a way that avoids these problems? *Homage to Eugene O'Neill* proposes an answer. It brings to the fore certain aspects of O'Neill, focuses on them, and develop them anew. It evokes and interacts with the old not by adopting a professorial distance, commenting in another voice, but by "channeling" the source of what it takes to have been O'Neill's works, speaking (so to speak) with his muse. It sets out to inhabit the same world as O'Neill's greater plays, without referring directly to them or parodying them. The reaction to the old is this act of resurrecting the same world, in the form of a play to be read. This, it might seem, doesn't make it a work of literary criticism, but instead another play. Many, perhaps all artworks, as we know from the literary criticism of the late twentieth century, echo, quote, and refer to each other: for a time the most-overused word at literary conferences was "intertextuality." Still, this is a play *to be read*, or at least offered in written form. Thus it is a written response to a written product, playing the role played in the last half-century by literary theory and criticism. But I suggest it is far more fun to read than most twentieth century literary theory and criticism, because closer to an artwork, or perhaps being one. That, finally, is the alteration of literary criticism this book points to: secondary literature "as" primary—or perhaps, the reverse.

This "new key" is, to be sure, a key so old it's new. It was last heard before Romanticism. To evoke M. H. Abrams's celebrated dichotomy, in *The Mirror and the Lamp*, of conflicting metaphors that stood, respectively, for the pre-Romantic and the Romantic artist, the neo-classical artist thought him- or herself to be mirroring Nature, rather than (as the later Romantics did) holding a lamp to illuminate Nature: the mirror could reflect anything, and did so indiscriminately. Nor was the action itself qualitatively different from other actions of other people in the world: the Artist, we might say in a Foucauldian strain, didn't exist; s/he hadn't been born yet. (Foucault thought s/he died somewhere in the mid-twentieth century.)

The Romantics offered a conception of the artist as a creator on par with, or at least walking in the footsteps of God the Father. This made the artistic act one that, though exalted, suddenly held an anomalous position in the world of the here and now: a position that needed explaining. (I've sketched the development of Romantic theory from neo-classical, and the various Modernisms from Romantic, in my *Modernism and its Discontents*.) Of course the question was: where does such an anomalous creature fit in? Enter theory and criticism, in the sense of an undertaking separable from the artwork in which we understand these today. No longer merely a person with a job, such as it seems even a prolific, successful composer like J.S. Bach thought himself, the artist expressed his or her vision—which extended beyond the purview of the ordinary person, making the artist like Victor Hugo's *mages* (wise men: in the poem "Les Mages"); the artist soared above those condemned to walk and was ungainly only when forced to walk about with them, like Baudelaire's albatross from the eponymous poem.

Justifying art

Movements arise as solutions to problems; so too do specific sorts of undertakings. Before Romanticism, we didn't have theory justifying and explaining art in the modern sense because art didn't need to be justified: the pre-Romantic mirror got its justification from being mimetic, showing things as they are—Aristotle, after all, had assured us that we got pleasure from seeing imitation. Classical and neo-classical writings about art take art for granted, describing rather than justifying. The problem Romanticism had to solve was this: what point had the lamp? Surely things didn't seem dark before it appeared? Why did we need the lamp at all?

One of the striking qualities of Romantic theory is that it was produced almost exclusively by poets, to justify in cosmic terms their own position in the world: Shelley's famous "poets are the unacknowledged legislators of the world" stands as typical of the early Romantic era. It's more than a little silly, or perhaps in retrospect sad, in that the rest of the world continued unaffected: the legislators were, it seemed, not only unacknowledged but also ineffective. So what kind of legislators were they?

Too, when people in the world got wind of the fact that artists actually considered themselves superior to the businessman, they became a bit indignant. The result was the great counter-swell of bourgeois taste, that hated thing of a Baudelaire, the "philistines" (as the British Romantics called them) who didn't appreciate artists. The philistines who failed to appreciate (or acknowledge) all these would-be legislators now seem to us to have been the result of a wave of Western prosperity produced in a certain class by the Industrial Revolution. We saw them again in the late twentieth century and now in the early twenty-first. If you're excited about your house and garden, or nowadays your electronic gadgets and your designer whatsits, you won't be looking for meaning in art; if you have a job in which you're Someone, you won't take kindly to being led from a darkness you didn't even know you were in.

The pushback by people so satisfied by their worldly possessions they didn't think of their state as being darkness at all, and hence not being in need of poetic illumination, produced the overwhelming tendency of the late nineteenth century to integrate literature and the arts into worldly pursuits. Literary criticism famously became "extrinsic," to use the term of the later

Modernist theorists René Welleck and Austin Warren, in their *Theory of Literature*, who were in their turn pushing back in a neo-Romantic vein against the Victorian pushback. In what the later Modernists saw as "extrinsic" criticism, literature was used as fragments of a larger biographical story about the writer, treated as an exemplary person, or as mines of moral lessons, or, in the later years of the nineteenth century, as fodder to feed theories of social conflict (Marxist analysis) or psychological theories (Freudian). The literary work wasn't thought of as inhabiting another realm; instead it was at most the highest layer of the here and now, something the bourgeoisie could aspire to, as painting was something to be hung in the well appointed home. What had happened to the separated artwork of Romanticism? It had, it seemed, all but disappeared.

To its rescue came the next wave of Romantics, those we call the Modernists, asserting once again that the world needed art, as the Formalist Shklovsky insisted in his celebrated essay "Art as Technique," "to make the stone stony."[1] Without art, it seemed, there was no perception of the world, or at least no perception save a very dull one. Though not all Modernists made this particular claim (Shelley had made s a similar assertion in his "Defense of Poetry" a century earlier), what strikes us now a century after the Modernists is the astonishing confidence of the Modernists, these neo-Romantics: their almost desperate insistence that they were *too* the center of the world, even as the fact that they had become a minority taste showed that they weren't.[2] (We should keep this moment in mind: the louder you have to assert something theoretically, the less likely it is that you've achieved it in fact.)

Brows

With Modernism comes the split between highbrow and low. In the Victorian era, every bourgeois family had a piano, on which the young ladies learned three songs by the composers who now have become hopelessly "highbrow." Nowadays classical music organizations fight for their lives and their audiences grow steadily grayer, while the lives of the vast majority are measured out in that year's pop songs. For the generations that have come and gone past Elvis Presley and the Beatles, music is a few chords that accompany bad poems.

Still, it's not clear that art in the Romantic sense was any more evenly spread about before Modernism; it's just that people danced—those who danced and to the extent they danced—to the tune of the highbrow. At the other end of the spectrum was the extremely lowbrow, say (to remain with the metaphor of dancing) at peasant weddings: lowbrow had its charm too; the tunes of the lowbrow were re-discovered by the Modernists seeking to break the lock of highbrow on the arts, and paintings of rustic peasants at their amusements decorated the houses of wealthy merchants and princes in the early Modern age. The twentieth century is clearly the victory of the popular middlebrow (to use a term of Virginia Woolf), itself lowbrow by the standards of say, late Beethoven quartets, things that everyone could appreciate. But would these people, the middlebrow, if suddenly transplanted to the Victorian era, suddenly be teaching their womenfolk Mendelssohn? Probably they would be doing nothing at all: pop music and photographic images break into new territory, fill a vacuum, rather than replacing or shunting aside something that was already there. And the historically brief attempt to spread high culture to the upwardly aspiring middle classes, as in the 1930s and 40s when even Broadway music was inflected by classical music, and "the balley" and "grand opera" were common touchstones of "class," seems in retrospect to have been a bubble destined to pop the larger, and hence thinner, it grew. Audiences for orchestral music are clearly diminished with respect to the 1960s. But are they smaller, relative to the general population, than (say) in 1815 Vienna?

Modernism has been revealed as the rearguard action of the threatened highbrow, a situation that led to its absurd bravado-saturated pronouncements. The over-confidence of Modernism is seen not only in the assertions of the Russian Formalists regarding their own necessity to the very act of perception, but also in the too-controlling purity of Le Corbusier's frigid "Unité d'Habitation,: part of his "Radiant City," a high-rise that, as Robert Hughes points out, people hated living in (oops; the architect-as-artist had forgotten about that part).[3] It's seen as well in Gertrude Stein's counter-intuitive insistence (in "Composition as Explanation," among other works) that the mere fact of being unappreciated in her own time meant she would be appreciated in another, and in T.S. Eliot's patrician assurance, in "Tradition and the Individual Talent," that new works controlled history, as they determined the way we read old—suggesting as it does that all history exists to culminate in T. S. Eliot.

Modernism claimed it controlled perception and offered the culmination of history. In retrospect its achievement was much more modest. Modernism, it now seems clear, was about the artist creating an alternative universe, and hence offered an intrinsically escapist aesthetic. Think of Joyce toiling away day after day on his so-complex tomes that took a lifetime to write, and to understand—that weren't meant to complement life as lived, but substitute for it. Certainly Proust replaced the living of his life by the writing of it. The artwork replaced life in fact, if not in theory—and frequently also in theory. After all Edmund Wilson, back at the beginning of it all, had written the first exploration of this "art in a new key," *Axel's Castle*. The character Axel comes from a play by the late Romantic French writer Villiers de l'Isle-Adam. Axel withdraws to within the confines of his castle, an "ivory tower" (apparently the first use of this phrase, here used without reference to the university), and notes that "as for living, our servants can do that for us." Wilson's point was that Modernism was based on a similarly escapist aesthetic: Modernism dreamed a beautiful dream, but the intensity of its proclamations was directly linked to the sacrifices necessary to keeping it alive.

Post-Modernism

Modernism was also the crucible of post-Modernism, which is writ inside it: many of Gertrude Stein's more disjointed texts seem quintessential post-Modernist texts; and "conceptual art," art that's not so interesting to see but very interesting to talk about—the gist of oeuvres such as that of Andy Warhol or even, arguably, Jasper Johns—like the theories of many of the Modernists that are more interesting than their artworks. Gertrude Stein's essays, as one example, are surprisingly easy to follow and end up being vastly more interesting than the output they were meant to justify, saving the reader the perceptual confusion of actually reading the works, with all of their meanders. Some readers have claimed the same for Virginia Woolf: *Jacob's Room* and *The Waves* are certainly more interesting as examples of what they're not than as examples of what they are; Woolf saw the problems of hierarchical plots clearly, but never really found a solution.[4] And many readers have found the works of James Joyce, or at least *Finnegans Wake*, so dense and so full of inside jokes we have to spend hours figuring out as to not be worth the trouble.

So too for Modernist architecture, and not merely that of Le Corbusier: it's more convincing as a model than when turned into a building and put into use. The Guggenheim Museum of Frank Lloyd Wright is interesting as a shape when seen from outside, but the spiral ramp that makes it so interesting is a horrible place to display art, forcing viewers to stand on an angle and forcing them inexorably down. And in the Geary-ized museum of the last decades, the building as artwork takes over from the smaller artworks inside: we no longer enter a building maintaining our integrity as individuals looking for works outside ourselves to react to. Instead, we are swallowed by the work, as if by a giant whale. The actions of the viewer inside such a monstrous mega-artwork seem as incidental as the gestures of the tiny pedestrians that would have swirled at the feet of the lurid fantasies of an Albert Speer. But of course such buildings aren't for the individuals coming to see things within them: they're for the town planners, the photographers of skyline shots they so enliven, the tourist board. Does opera sound better inside the now-iconic Sydney opera house? That's not the point. At least inside, it's still just a hall.

Modernism too contains all the post-Modernist love of pastiche as artistic expression: taking from others, then claiming that the act of re-presenting is itself the creative act. T. S. Eliot, in "The Waste Land," and other Modernists such as Ezra Pound, made clear that quotation was itself a means of self-expression. Collage and appropriation became mainstream with the works of Picasso, Gris, and Braque: newspapers are painted or incorporated into paintings; Dada incorporated the world of trash. In a Picasso statue in the Hirshhorn Museum in Washington, D.C., a bowl becomes the belly of a pregnant woman, an oddly broken receptacle the face of an infant whose arms are curving pipes; Duchamp at least turned a urinal upside-down to make it into "Fountain" as one of his "ready-mades," but the bristling bottle-drying rack was presented neat: the one on view in the Philadelphia Museum was "re-created" in the 1960s, signed twice with two dates by the artist. And the world outside was mined too by other artists for interesting shapes: "primitive" art, outsider art (such as the art of children and schizophrenics)—all was shaped in interestingly different ways, and could be offered to spectators hungry for the new.

This act of simply re-presenting the world in an act has become central to post-Modernist art. As I write, an exhibit of the photographs of Richard Prince, themselves photographic details of billboard advertising photographs, fill the Guggenheim. What's new in the works of Prince (for so we insist they are: works of Prince, not works of the advertising photographer whom he, in his turn, photographed the works of) is the focus, the frame, the presentation, the fact that we're meant to notice just this part of the world that already exists, and that in fact has already been signed by another "artist." Or we can sign the unsigning. Back in 1953 Robert Rauschenberg presented a drawing by Willem de Kooning that he,

Rauschenberg, had erased—the erasure, though not total, was the artistic statement, and the work presented as "by" Rauschenberg, not de Kooning. (The title was "Erased de Kooning Drawing.") Sometimes what's being signed hasn't been previously signed: in the 1980s Joseph Beuys filled glass cases with fat; galleries show great fiber or felt constructions hanging from the walls onto the floor that make us aware of the "texture of the raw material," as museum guides will assure us.

Whole art galleries after the turn of the millennium are filled with such acts of re-presenting: the average footsore tourist sees them, correctly, as "technique"-poor. "My dog could do that," many of them say. "My three-year-old could do that." Could, of course, in terms of capability, but of course wouldn't: no dog or three-year-old would understand the implications of doing this or putting this in a museum. From the point of view of the tourist, understandably, this justification for putting the object in a museum is circular: the tourist asks for another reason to justify the work being in a museum; the answer cannot merely be that the fact that it's there justifies its being there. And yet that is the answer given: what's in the museum doesn't look any different (perhaps) than something a dog could do, but the fact that it's in a museum shows it is. The tourist takes the museum for granted.

Contemporary art seems to tourists technique-poor, as in fact it is. Artists no longer distinguish themselves by technique, by being able to perform actions we can't do, only by offering products we don't. We were asked to see the physical act of throwing paint on huge canvases in sweeping flings of Abstract Expressionism as part of the nature of the painting: the art isn't the product, it's the process of making it. Many contemporary works seem like huge chunks of the world—performance art, conceptual art—ripped from their surrounds and signed: we're supposed to take the chunk of the world as belonging not to us but to the artist, and be grateful to him or her for having offered it back to us.[5] The closed loop of art has now become absolute—at least from within the loop. The fact is, however, that it isn't closed at all: we have only to leave the museum to find the world again, unprocessed. Why should we go to a museum to appreciate the fiber or the wood being offered back to us when we are surrounded by fiber and wood, and can notice these things on our own, and without paying homage to a middleman? But of course pointing out we can do this threatens the livelihood (such as it is) of the middleman, or –woman, and so must be resisted as a naïve reaction, something showing ignorance of the way things work.

Critical lessons

The critical theory of the second half of the twentieth century in America was inspired by the Modernist artists' desperate assertion of their own artistic necessity ("art makes the stone stony"): critical theory, until that point seen as a handmaid when not practiced by the poets themselves, struck out on its own. The Anglo-American New Criticism developed its own jargon ("irony," "ambiguity") and the related insistence that criticism had to be done in a certain way, "intrinsic" (to return to Welleck and Warren's dichotomy) to the text.

For some decades, roughly the 40s and 50s, the relationship of this quasi-independent way of doing criticism to the primary text was still, at least nominally, one of servant to master—it was still accepted by almost all that the texts in question were two, a primary text and a secondary one. The next step had to be, logically, the assertion that the servant was fully the equal of the master. This happened in American criticism with the arrival of structuralism, and then deconstructionism, from France. Instead of reading the text, we read the theory, which englobes and in some cases overwhelms the text. Roland Barthes's *S/Z*, a too-much-read book of marginalia on a Balzac short story where we're meant to read both the now-cut-into-fragments story and the fragmentary comments, inspired a generation of graduate students. Students might not be Balzac, but then again, why bother to try? They could be Barthes, and Barthes had swallowed Balzac.

It's difficult for us now to see the lure of, say, Lévi-Strauss's "semiotic squares" for interpreting pretty nearly everything, part of the structuralist phase to which Langer, in her own way, belonged.[6] And perhaps they had no intrinsic lure: they were, however, complex, in a new vocabulary, and discussing them was guaranteed to keep out the uninitiated, who were pushed away even further upon the arrival of such exotic terminology as "*différence*," *mise-en-abîme*, and *écriture*, all kept tantalizingly in the French of the so-Parisian Derrida, and reeking, it seemed, of the cigarette smoke of the Left Bank cafés. Derridean theory, based on switching of the usual valences, was clever in the hands of Derrida, a sort of "gotcha" gadfly position that grew heavy as it crossed the Atlantic, not a dart to prick but a club to annihilate. For Derrida, all intuition was false: presence, it turned out, was not more fundamental than absence, which in turn meant that the written text, with its famously absent author, was primary over speech. Commentary on text was no longer commentary on text, it was itself the text. And there was nothing outside the text.

In this way, the discipline of literary theory—as something one could get a degree in, and teach—came into its own in America in the 1970s and 1980s. Criticism of the journalistic kind was passé. During these years too the humanities in America were institutionalizing their methodology, regularizing humanistic studies using science as a paradigm. Instead of reading or considering literature, we now did "research" on "texts": what literature professors did was fully as specialized as what scientists did—though, paradoxically, all readings of literature were held to be not objective, as science held its own achievements, but instead subjective, the result of belonging to a certain social group. There might not be such things as facts, but this precisely was the truth that the insiders shared when they met.

And meet they did. A priestly class and an insider vocabulary implies confabs in which to be priestly and insider together. Langer makes the point in *Philosophy in a New Key* that though an effluence of conferences around a certain topic seems to show the vigorous good health of that way of thinking, in fact it shows only that an era is coming to an end: soon that vocabulary will be exhausted, as people will tire of it.[7] In the 1990s the American academic landscape was thick with conferences where the initiated met to speak the common language: countless professors and graduate students burnt up countless gallons of airline gasoline getting to places where they could be with those who spoke the same language.

The enterprise remained constant; only the precise content changed. In their turn, the Derrideans were replaced by the Foucauldians: the shift went from focus on a world of texts removed from contact with the world and endlessly commenting on each other, to the insistence that texts not only related to the world, texts created the world. The two positions are logically related, of course.

The Foucauldians, disciples of Michel Foucault—another thinker who, logically speaking should never have had disciples (his points were clear the first time and worked better in the hands of the person who invented them), insisted that the West oppressed the Rest not, as we might think, through economic and military power, but through our presentation of them in our texts. It was a stunning claim, one that made professors feel that they were at the center of things, even if in a negative way: at least, when they atoned, it was for something large, the subjugation of the entire world. This was the last turn of the post-Romantic wheel, this final try to prove Shelley right that "poets are the unacknowledged legislators of the world"—though authors here of the world's problems. The position claimed for writers still reeks of importance, even if its effect is nefarious rather than salutary, and requires wearing a hair shirt. Every reading of literature is merely a specific, group-determined reading. Each reading implies all those it isn't.

But suddenly, in the new millennium, the fir trees are producing too many pinecones—to return to Langer's point: lots of pine cones on trees isn't a sign of health any more than lots of conferences is a sign of intellectual health. In trees it means the forests are under stress from acid rain; in the intellectual world the fact that everybody is doing it means that the vocabulary of the few has been democratized, taken up by the many. If works are really the expression of group privilege, the uncomfortable fact is that there are suddenly too many groups trying to get their fifteen minutes on center stage. If works of literature further the interests of merely the sub-group to which their author belongs, and universities try to hire one of each, they will soon be caught in a dialogue of the deaf, with each representative of a neglected group looking out only for the interests of his or her group—and of course, being reviled in their turn as new groups turn up demanding their representation.

What do we do now?

What comes next? I suggest: an attempt to get beyond the Romantic split, that dangerous step into the abyss that claimed so much for the creator it became incumbent to re-integrate him once again into a larger framework—which framework became the very content of Romantic theory. (I've tried such a step back to before the Romantics in *An Essay in Post-Romantic Theory*.) We've exhausted the capital produced by Romanticism. The only way forward is to go back—in this case, to texts that are no more creative than critical, with no special status being claimed for the first, and hence no disdain expressed for the second. The next stage of evolution of literary criticism, therefore, is its disappearance as a separate discipline, and its re-integration into the forms it once commented on.

Others of my texts straddle the line between didactic and creative, or insist that there is no difference. When I sent a piece of mine called "The Autobiography of Gertrude Stein," the story of a man who visited Gertrude Stein in the 1920s written in modified Steinese, to a journal, the editor called to find out how old I was. Was this my autobiography? If so he'd publish it as an essay. Being assured I was a younger man, and a writer, he called it a story, and published it as such. Another of my pieces started life as a series of poems; I re-lined them as prose, and at an editor's suggestion put as a title of each the one or two writers referred to in the piece. I gave the whole the title of "A Student's Guide to the Classics." I think it was classified as an essay. But is it essay? Story? Prosy poems? I don't know.

Long texts
Homage to Eugene O'Neill is an extremely long text, longer than *Strange Interlude* or *A Long Day's Journey Into Night*: this is part of its homage. It adds to *Strange Interlude*'s nine acts another multiple of three to bring the total to an even dozen, divided between two main parts, as in O'Neill. This fact, among other things, determines its nature as primarily a written work: it fulfils its destiny in being printed, and though any text can be performed, does not aim ever to leave the page. *Strange Interlude* was originally presented with time for theater-goers to go out for dinner; it seems unlikely they'd tolerate going out for multiple meals rather than merely one—nor is the human concentration span, or the human behind, meant to sit still and concentrate for that long. (The all-night popular dramas of Southeast Asia aren't meant to be paid attention to in this way: one eats, sleeps, and talks, much perhaps as the audience in the pre-modern West did at the theater.) And so, though inspired by the stage, it transcends the stage, and ends up back in a book. Readers can take as long as they like, and need not "pay attention"—as the Romantic and then Modernist work demands they do—uninterruptedly. The work ceases to demand the attention of the viewer or reader, save insofar as s/he wishes to give that attention. It's as if the constructions of felt had come out of the museum, perhaps like James Smithson's "earthworks."

Length is part of the essence here, as in O'Neill. *Strange Interlude* goes on and on, adding event to event to stretch the whole out to something like a generation. As a result, what it expresses most fundamentally is the taste of the passage of time: a person's life, seen as it unrolls, takes odd turns that the person living the life hadn't foreseen. Seen from without, a life may have a predictable shape; seen from within, it's clear it was all being made up as we went along.

Like *Strange Interlude*, *Homage to Eugene O'Neill* revolves around a central female character who ages from girlhood to adulthood. O'Neill's heroine was Nina; mine is Barbara. I've stretched Barbara's maturation out to fifty years, as opposed to O'Neill's twenty, to emphasize even further all the changes that occur in the course of a single life—and to make clear that each generation is replaced by the next, and that by the next, and so on—

making risible the pretension of the Aristotelian drama to a clear shape in life: even if one person achieves it, the flow continues overlapping into the next generation, and then the next, and then the next. And what shape does this new thing make except a bumpy string, always longer than it is high or low?

What characterizes O'Neill's longer dramas too is their deadly seriousness. At each moment we feel the playwright's conscious attempt to write the Great American Play, something we rarely attempt any longer. In the 20s and 30s of the last century, by contrast, such an attempt seemed just the ticket. As a result, O'Neill wasn't afraid to attempt a *gravitas* that now seems old-fashioned. *Homage to Eugene O'Neill* attempts this *gravitas* as well, not as parody or post-Modern reference, but as homage, an attempt to re-inhabit and recall to life a perhaps otherwise vanished sensibility. Perhaps, in order to achieve it, we need only attempt it with no sense of apology?

For O'Neill, it was conceivable that whole life could be blighted, say by an early death in war, or , echoing Aeschylus in *Mourning Becomes Electra*, by a family curse. The trajectory of the passage of time in *Homage to Eugene O'Neill* seems to the family members to be fate working itself out as well. The family rises and falls as a result of the decisions of its females, who wonder at the end if things could ever have been different. Yet for *Homage to Eugene O'Neill*, the central truth hovering over all is that though each step we take leads to the next, the whole of our life is ever so much different than we expected: we turn out to have been a different person than we knew. Time itself determines who we are, which is to say: what life we lead. The epic sweep of O'Neill's longer works is itself their greatest contribution to literature. Sometimes we sense that that O'Neill does better with the big picture than the small. The individual events that make up his sweeping passages of time seem not grave, but perhaps a bit overwrought. Their expression too sometimes seems melodramatic: deprived of the momentum of context in their plays, many of the characters' speeches seem a bit wooden, too "stagy." How, we wonder, could we imagine anyone actually saying this? In *Homage to Eugene O'Neill*, the epic is more domestic, the work a sort of "chamber epic"—and, as a result, the speeches of necessity more believable, less histrionic. The page offers a dish best eaten cold, not hot, as in the theater. Its givens are different, as the givens of the movie screen require a different acting style than the theater, where grimaces and gestures must play to the back balcony.

Yet O'Neill was clearly aware that what he portrayed was melodrama rather than tragedy, as if even for him the reaching for *gravitas* was a posture, the gesture itself the most tragic element of his great melodramas. And perhaps the overwrought nature of many of the utterances was the result of his turning this knob up too high *on purpose*. O'Neill's title in the case of *Strange Interlude* comes from Nina musing that "our lives are merely strange, dark interludes in the electrical displays of God the Father." All that we have experienced, hours on the stage interrupted by dinner, was nothing but one such interlude, an echo of Lamartine's notion (popularized by Liszt as a title for his work *Les Préludes*) that "life is a series of preludes to the dance of death." "Electrical displays" in the heavens make a lot of noise and violent light and actually amount to very little, a natural form of Shakespeare's "sound and fury signifying nothing." And "displays" of any kind are by nature hollow, all showing and no meaning. O'Neill, ultimately, falls short of tragedy—but probably knew this about himself, since he doesn't seem to have thought life amounted to too much. His works are high camp rather than tragedy, melodrama rather than drama; the mannered nature of many of his speeches perhaps the result of this sense that overwrought was at least interesting. Yet all this, both the attempt and the falling short, is the source of the pathos of his greater works, a sensation too deep for tears: what we see all goes on so long, the emotions they evoke are so extreme, but to what end?

Like *Strange Interlude*, thus, *Homage to Eugene O'Neill* is melodrama, sometimes of the most shameless sort. Central to the melodrama of O'Neill's play is the fact that it revolves around the shocking-for-the 1920s notion of abortion and bearing the child of a man not one's husband. *Homage to Eugene O'Neill* plays with this notion without deciding whether it's happened, and adds to the mixture miscarriage, illegitimacy, and homosexuality, along with marital infidelity. In *Strange Interlude*, the war victim is the husband-to-be; here it's the son. In *Strange Interludes*, the son is gifted and powerful, and doesn't know who his father is; in the present work, the son is less gifted, and does know, but doesn't really like the situation.

If the muse of *Strange Interlude* is the loudest voice here, the muse of O'Neill's "Greek" works, such as *Mourning Becomes Electra*, is heard as well. Barbara, the central character in *Homage to Eugene O'Neill*, wonders if she is carrying out a family curse and is much taken with a course in Greek tragedy she's taken at Bryn Mawr. O'Neill has as his heroine the daughter of a professor at an Ivy-style college; here she's one of a family line of Sister School graduates, and it's her daughter who becomes the professor. Like the Greek dramas, *Homage to Eugene O'Neill* places the bloodiest events offstage: what we see onstage is their for- or after-shocks, where we can pay attention to how the people articulate, rather than to the horrific thing that has happened.

In *Homage to Eugene O'Neill* are also hints of *Long Day's Journey Into Night*, which is to the neo-classical five-act play as Mahler's symphonies are to the classical symphony of Haydn or Mozart. *Long Day's Journey* is structurally the flip side of *Strange Interlude*, a kind of Greek re-working of a Romantic plot, with everything the family has been workout out through years becoming clear in a single day. Probably because its framework is so tight, respecting the Aristotelian unities of time and place, the first act of *Long Day's Journey*, like the longer movements of Mahler, is so laden with its own byways and flyways that we almost lose sight of where it fits into the whole—and is long enough to be a conventional play, if we'd only break it off there. Seen as an end in itself, in fact, Act I of *Long Day's Journey Into Night* produces a sense not unlike that of reading the meanderings of Stein that every moment of life has its own weight, its own taste. Life doesn't get wrapped up, after all: the fact that each character in *Long Day's Journey* has his or her tawdry secret is one of the least attractive aspects of the work, being too neat, the well-made plot taking over despite attempts to exclude it. Some O'Neill plays founder on this "everyone has a secret" rock; *The Iceman Cometh* (who can entitle a play like this nowadays?) is the most egregious.

Despite the formally inverse natures of *Long Day's Journey* and *Strange Interlude,* the two plays are more like than unlike. The forces in both are more centrifugal than centripetal: the texture of life is the central subject of both, not the artificial forming necessary to its portrayal on the stage. *Homage to Eugene O'Neill* attempts to break the grip of this forming impulse through its very length, and the fact that the forming of each of the individual acts is as a dramatic high point seen through scare quotes, like an episode of soap operas from daytime television. The wobbly organ music rises, the actors look meaningfully at each other—and the logo of the program appears.

Homage to Eugene O'Neill charts the rise and fall of a family—at least when seen from the perspective of the heroine, Barbara: and yet the next generation takes things as they are for granted, and continues on, perhaps even to rise again: the "beginning, middle and end" of Aristotle unravels as time adds yet other beginnings, overlapping middles with ends and with even newer beginnings. Its structure is thus not tragic but, in the Brechtian sense, epic: O'Neill strove for the tragic in his content, yet his impulse seems to be to the epic. *Homage to Eugene O'Neill* gives in to this impulse.

To be sure, the end of *Homage to Eugene O'Neill* is the shrouded-with-memories, nothing-is-ever-possible-again world of *Long Day's Journey*, with the heroine back in the house she'd left when the family fortunes began to rise, back before the fall. "And then I married James Tyrone," we can almost imagine Barbara saying. "And was happy, for a time." Yet this is only *her* world; her daughter lives in another world entirely and has long ago escaped this house. To Sarah, Barbara's life is all but irrelevant, and to her grandson it is unknown: nothing is ever wrapped up forever, life is just one thing after another. *Homage to Eugene O'Neill* senses this lesson in O'Neill, and makes it clearer.

The aspect of *Strange Interlude* that struck audiences strongest, and the aspect that has proven problematic in performance—so that this play in its own way was an early example of a work most essentially meant to be read—is its use of articulated thoughts, a Wagnerian form of the Shakespearean soliloquy, broken up into continuous commentary rather than isolated off in the form of self-sufficient operatic "arias." As speeches where nobody seems to be paying attention, in Shakespeare, they don't bother actors or directors much. In *Strange Interlude*, where others are possibly meant to freeze while we hear a character's thoughts, they seem odd. So odd, in fact, that when the same well is plumbed, as for *Homage to Eugene O'Neill*, what comes up is another form of this aspect: extensive use of "naturalistic" versions of this same device. Barbara reads her own letter aloud to herself; her father dictates to a recording device and her mother talks on the telephone. And in one scene Nadine, Barbara's mother, articulates out loud not what she's thinking as she writes a letter but what she would say if she were to write the truth rather than the socially acceptable letter she is in fact composing, all alone, on a stage with no one else present: we're not hearing her thoughts, we're getting a commentary she'd never give.

Characters

Homage to Eugene O'Neill takes place in Tyler City, North Carolina, a medium-large city, during the fifty years from 1939 to 1989. The characters are three groups of two, each group from a different generation (1) NADINE and STANLEY Rush, whose (2) daughter BARBARA marries MARTIN Kreuzinger and has two children, (3) SARAH and TOMMY. By the end of the play TOMMY has a son, who does not appear.

First Generation NADINE and STANLEY Rush. Vary in age from ca. 40 to ca. 60.

Second Generation BARBARA Rush, later Kreuzinger. When seen first, she is 16 (though referred to when younger); when seen last, a woman of close to 60. MARTIN Kreuzinger, first appears at ca. 30, last seen at ca. 60.

Third Generation SARAH Kreuzinger, seen from ca. 20 to mid 30s. TOMMY Kreuzinger, seen from ca. 17 to 27.

List of acts

Part I

Act One. 1939. NADINE and STANLEY. The porch of their first house.

Act Two. 1945. First BARBARA, then NADINE, each alone. Two rooms in the larger Rush house.

Act Three. 1948. BARBARA and STANLEY. STANLEY's office, President of Tyler City Chemical Corp.

Act Four. 1950. The living room of the Rush house. First NADINE, alone. Then STANLEY, NADINE, and BARBARA.

Act Five. 1950; the day after Scene Four. A park bench. BARBARA and MARTIN.

Act Six. 1954. The library in the Rush house. STANLEY and MARTIN, then MARTIN and BARBARA.

Part II

Act Seven. 1967. The kitchen in the Kreuzinger house. MARTIN, BARBARA.

Act Eight. 1972. The library/study in the Kreuzinger house. MARTIN, BARBARA, TOMMY.

Act Nine. 1975. The living room of the Kreuzinger house. MARTIN and BARBARA.

Act Ten. 1980. A park bench. SARAH, MARTIN.

Act Eleven. 1982. The living room of TOMMY's house. TOMMY, SARAH.

Act Twelve. 1989. The library in the large Rush house. BARBARA, SARAH.

Synopsis

In the first generation, NADINE—who has been raised to wealth but lost it through her father's suicide—pressures her more reticent husband, STANLEY, to diversify his father's fertilizer business in order to make profits from the expected war. The profits are made and NADINE is once again wealthy, but STANLEY is relegated to a figurehead position in the firm and begins to drink. Their son, Mark, who may be the issue of an affair between NADINE and her husband's business partner, is killed in the war, and NADINE is consumed with guilt. Their daughter, BARBARA, who as an adolescent was close to both her father and brother, finishes college at Bryn Mawr, where her mother has gone, and marries MARTIN, a hard-working young man whom she pressures to go into the family business, by now a major industrial concern. MARTIN acquiesces for a time, but soon leaves the company to go into politics. The announcement that he is going to strike out on his own because Tyler City Chemicals is riddled with corruption causes BARBARA—who already has a daughter, SARAH, after a pregnancy marked by bleeding and complications—to have a miscarriage. BARBARA is convinced the child would have been a boy.

MARTIN is elected mayor of Tyler City, and he and BARBARA celebrate. SARAH goes Bryn Mawr, and TOMMY—the child BARBARA had after her miscarriage—breaks the news that he has gotten his girlfriend pregnant. TOMMY is not so promising intellectually as SARAH, but he feels close to MARTIN. MARTIN arranges an abortion, which TOMMY both accepts and simultaneously resents. Years pass. BARBARA arrives home to find MARTIN standing before certain disgrace; he is about to resign as mayor as the result of an investigation into influence-peddling. MARTIN admits to having taken bribes in order to get money for his mistress, whom he says he loves. BARBARA leaves him. The one member of the family who remains close to MARTIN after his disgrace is SARAH, who has become a lawyer and later a professor. She tells her father her own love interest is a woman in Heidelberg, and that it is therefore unlikely that she will be giving him a grandchild. TOMMY by this time is living with a woman by whom he has a son named Billy. This common-law wife is a coke addict and a thief. TOMMY and his sister butt heads over the situation. The last scene takes place the day of MARTIN's death. SARAH goes to visit BARBARA, now living back in her parents' old house They note that there is some hope for the family in Billy, who by now is living with his father alone. The play ends with BARBARA turning back to her television, and telling SARAH not to pity her.

PART I

ACT ONE

1939. The sound of crickets. A man and woman, the man about 40, the woman slightly younger, are sitting on a bench as if on a porch, but not touching each other. They are STANLEY and NADINE Rush. Their accents betray that STANLEY has grown up south of the Mason-Dixon Line, and NADINE well to its north.

STANLEY: Barbara certainly went to bed early. I can't remember the last time we just sat here listening to the crickets.

NADINE (a bit anxiously): I hope Mark is all right.

STANLEY: Of course he's all right. When I was his age I was hauling sacks of fertilizer for my father. I was so tired when I went to bed I didn't know whether I was on a mattress or not. Sleeping in the open with the Boy Scouts is luxury by comparison.

NADINE: Maybe he's listening to the crickets too.

STANLEY: He's probably asleep.

NADINE (giving up, turning to other things She is silent for several moments.): There were crickets in the mountains, outdoors, in the summer. Before Daddy died and I went to Aunt Martha. She was the one who told me he'd killed himself. To make it clear to me how grateful I should be to her that she had taken me in. The witch. [Turning to STANLEY] I haven't complained too much about those times, have I?

STANLEY: Not more than they deserved, probably.

[Pause; sound of crickets]

NADINE: It took all day to get there from New York. The leather upholstery in the car was so smooth. There was a little vase hanging inside for flowers. Daddy always kept a rose in it. Roses were Mother's favorite flower. Daddy always said it was because her name was Rose. I've told you that.

STANLEY (patiently; has heard all this before): Yes.

NADINE (ruefully): I'm not sure I even remember her. Oh, fleeting things, like the smell of her hair. Not what she looked like.

STANLEY: But you have that picture on the mantel.

NADINE: When I close my eyes I see the picture, so it's the picture I'm remembering, not her. It's like thinking you're looking out a window, and then realizing it's really a painting propped up against a wall. Like drawing down the curtain in front of a window: a sense of disappointment, of loss. [Pause.] I remember the long drive, the way I would look out at the scenery. The chauffeur sat up front. Daddy would read the paper. The governess, Miss Carter her name was, would knit.

STANLEY: My poor little rich girl.

NADINE: You can joke about it, but it was all too true. There was the upstairs maid, the downstairs maid, the cook, the butler, the chauffeur. And many gardeners. And me, all alone. [Change of tone; brisker.] But at the cottage things were different. Daddy would spend the day fishing and I would go exploring down to the lake and into the woods. He had a moustache, and dark hair. In the evening he and I would sit on the porch and listen to the crickets, and the cry of the loons.

STANLEY: No loons around Tyler City. None that I know of, anyway.

NADINE: But lots of crickets.

STANLEY: And darkness.

NADINE (pause): Yes. Darkness.

STANLEY (suddenly bitter): Sometimes I want to escape.

NADINE (treating it as a joke): Tyler City is escape enough.

STANLEY: You say nothing ever happens here.

NADINE (suddenly coquettish): One thing did. That Christmas I came down to spend the holidays with Millie Chesterton. The Christmas I met you.

STANLEY (sidestep): Whatever happened to Millie?

NADINE: I ran into Mrs. Chesterton just last week. She said Millie is still in Chicago. She married her Princeton man. You remember.

STANLEY (vaguely): Oh yes.

NADINE: They have three children. [Pause.] I hardly have any contact with her. [Pause.] To be frank, I don't know what I'd say to her if I did. I can't really admit you still just sell fertilizer.

STANLEY [blocking this out]: That first day, you wore a long white dress.

NADINE: Nonsense. It was yellow. Knee-length. I was trying to look like a flapper.

STANLEY: Yellow?

NADINE: You wore a black suit.

STANLEY (continuing nostalgic): I couldn't believe you married me. Me, the owner of a fertilizer store with a high school education. You, a Bryn Mawr girl.

NADINE (half-teasing him): No accounting for feelings.

STANLEY (agreeing): No accounting for feelings.

NADINE: Your mother never did approve of your marrying a Yankee. But I think I've managed to fit in. Haven't I?

STANLEY: You live here, that's about all I can say.

NADINE: I belong to the Garden Club, I belong to the Ladies Auxiliary of the Lion's Club, and Maybelle Porter even said she was going to sponsor me for the Flowers of the Confederacy next year.

STANLEY: Even though your great-granddaddy was practically Sherman's right hand man on his march to the sea.

NADINE: Which you're never going to tell Maybelle.

STANLEY: She won't hear it from me.

NADINE (conspiratorially): Let's hope they don't investigate.

[Silence; a moment of consonance.]

STANLEY (musing): It isn't possible Mark is thirteen. My little girl almost ten.

NADINE (the consonance fading): We've managed to hang on, haven't we? Despite everything?

STANLEY: You always said I was solid and predictable.

NADINE (quietly): Too predictable. I hear you're about to miss a real chance.

STANLEY: What's Ethel been telling you? Jim shouldn't pass on all these things to her. Women have no business in business.

NADINE (trying to be light): That's what you always say.

STANLEY (revving up an old speech): Business is for men, like drinking whiskey and smoking cigars. Of course, I can't help what Jim Masterson tells Ethel. He comes from Baltimore and has different ideas. [He looks at her, as if repentant.] Now you've made me be unkind.

NADINE: Which is against the code of a gentleman, as we all know.

STANLEY (with as much dignity as he can muster): It is.

NADINE: Some women nowadays drink whiskey.

STANLEY (playing along): Yes, but very few of them smoke cigars.

NADINE: Somehow that seems hardly to prove your point.

STANLEY (lighter): My mother did warn me about marrying a Yankee girl. Always have to get the better of a discussion with their husbands.

NADINE: I want to know what chance it is Jim sees. You know he was always the better businessman of you two.

STANLEY: You've told me often enough. [Half-ironic, half-conciliatory] Of course, you'd have been better than either of us.

NADINE: If we didn't live in this ridiculous world of yours where "women have no business in business," I'd have proved it to you long ago.

STANLEY (not rising to the bait): Maybe you should tell me what Ethel said.

NADINE: Jim thinks you can make a lot of money.

STANLEY: Is that what she says?

NADINE: And that you're dragging your heels. [Pause; no response.] Is it true?

STANLEY (not taking the bait): What am I supposed to say to that?

NADINE: It *is* true, isn't it? I thought you were destined for great things. [Bitterly] It took me a while, but finally I realized you had no ambition at all.

STANLEY (still unruffled): Be realistic. You knew what the business was when I took it over from father. Just a small-time fertilizer store.

NADINE (changing tack, encouragingly): Yes, and you've done very well with it. You produce now as well as sell.

STANLEY (ironically): Now I process cow dung as well as sell it. [Turning on her, defiantly] It's good enough for me.

NADINE (insisting): What's Jim's plan?

STANLEY: Why don't you ask him? Or Ethel?

NADINE: Wouldn't you rather tell me?

STANLEY (wearily, giving in): Fertilizers use chemicals. Jim thinks that with some investment, we could turn around what we're doing to involve production of chemicals.

NADINE: Is there a future in that?

STANLEY: If there's war, chemicals will be very important.

NADINE: Important?

STANLEY: Lucrative. Money-making.

NADINE: What a wonderful opportunity! Is war likely?

STANLEY: There will be war. Or rather, there already is one. Hitler has invaded Czechoslovakia, after all. England is arming. The United States will certainly be drawn in.

NADINE (excited and trying to make a joke): Czechoslovakia. That's one that I never could spell.

STANLEY (playing along): Even with your Bryn Mawr degree?

NADINE: Even with my Bryn Mawr degree. But Jim's plan. It sounds foolproof!

STANLEY: Well, I guess I'm a fool. I don't like the idea. And we don't need the money. Anyway, it's not the way a Southerner would do things.

NADINE: It sounds as if we could be rich again!

STANLEY: I was never rich.

NADINE (fiercely): When you're rich, people can't tell you what to do.

STANLEY: You're the one telling me what to do.

NADINE (trying to be positive): I thought we were making progress when you went into production.

STANLEY (bitterly): With the money you got when we married.

NADINE: You've always been so defensive about that.

STANLEY: A man likes to feel he's made it on his own.

NADINE (again trying the carrot rather than the stick): You have made it on your own. Without your hard work, the business wouldn't have done half as well. And anyway, it was so little, the money. Just a bit that Daddy had put aside so the creditors couldn't touch it.

STANLEY: Little for you, a lot for me. That's what let me expand. And take in Jim as a partner, you remember.

NADINE: You see, it *was* useful. And yet you've resented it. Without me, we'd be nowhere. We wouldn't even have what we have.

STANLEY: That's my point, dear. I feel as if I'd only been along for the ride. First with my father. Now you.

NADINE (frustrated): If Jim thinks we could make a fortune, how could you be against that?

STANLEY: It means branching out into something I don't really know anything about. Jim does, of course. He went to college.

NADINE (downplaying): Yes. He went to college.

STANLEY (pedantically): I have no interest in changing the fundamental nature of this company. [Appealing to her.] I've been in fertilizer all my life. That's all I know about.

NADINE: You've let opportunities pass you by. We live in the same house we lived in when we married. We live the same life.

STANLEY: What's wrong with that? All I wanted was to come home to you every night, to watch the years go by.

NADINE: The years go by whatever you do.

STANLEY: Going into chemicals involves a huge loan. And that entails some risk. Did Ethel tell you that?

NADINE (momentarily checked): Well, I knew the money had to come from somewhere.

STANLEY: Did she tell you we'd have to put up the business itself as collateral? Everything my father every worked for would be on the line. Everything I ever worked for.

NADINE: But if there's sure to be a war—

STANLEY: You have a son. What if he's killed?

NADINE: The war can't go on that long.

STANLEY: The last one went on a while.

NADINE: Where's your sense of patriotism? You used to regret that you were too young for the last war.

STANLEY: One minute you're telling me how much money we're going to make, and the next minute you're talking about patriotism. It's one thing to defend your country in her hour of need, and another to go looking for trouble.

NADINE: If it's going to happen, we might as well get in on it.

STANLEY: For years, Jim has been pushing me to expand, take chances, move into new things. And so have you.

NADINE: You always *were* defensive.

STANLEY (for whom the issue is decided): Leave the business to me. You'll be happier in the long run.

NADINE (reflectively): Happy?

STANLEY (hesitating a moment before plunging in): If we're not happy, my business decisions are hardly the cause of it.

NADINE (suddenly watchful): What do you mean?

STANLEY (deciding to speak): You don't think things are going well, do you?

NADINE: Is that a question I'm supposed to answer?

STANLEY: I mean between us.

NADINE (faintly): Us?

STANLEY (suddenly turning on her): You're frigid.

NADINE: Good heavens.

STANLEY: There. I've been wanting to say that for years.

NADINE (pause): Maybe just with you.

STANLEY (self-righteous): A man has needs, after all.

NADINE: Needs or no needs, you don't expect me to go to bed with you when I know you've been running around with someone else. After a while, you even stopped trying to hide it from me. Did you think I didn't know?

STANLEY: You're not pretending you're innocent?

NADINE: Not this all over again. Dear God.

STANLEY (heedless; this is part of his speech): I was in Tennessee nine months before. But eight months before, I was back. So of course when Mark was born eight months later, he had to be premature. Only he wasn't. The doctor told me he was a full-term baby. And look at him now. I've never seen a healthier boy.

NADINE: The doctor also explained to you that eight months can be a full-term baby. You just wanted an excuse to run around.

STANLEY (changing the subject): You and your dreams of making me into your father, with his bankrupt steel mill and his suicide. That's what you should be remembering from your childhood.

NADINE (shocked that he has gone this far): Stanley!

STANLEY: I think I have a normal amount of ambition. Or I did, anyway. You killed it, with your endless pushing. You have to know when to let go of a horse's mouth, you know, or he'll throw you.

NADINE: Are you throwing me?

STANLEY: Mark isn't mine.

NADINE: I know, he's Jim's. You've always been convinced of that.

STANLEY: You're saying it, not me.

NADINE: You could be the partner of a man who had a child by your wife?

STANLEY: Business is business. It's separate from home life.

NADINE: Ask Jim.

STANLEY: He'll deny it. I would too, in his place.

NADINE: You've never loved Mark.

STANLEY: I wish I could have loved him more.

NADINE (flatly): It wasn't Jim.

STANLEY: Who was it, then?

NADINE: The night you got back from Tennessee you broke the lamp trying to get at me. That was what conceived Mark, not an affair with your partner. I've told you. Many times.

STANLEY: I'll never know, will I?

NADINE: You poor stupid man. All this an excuse to justify your behavior. I wish you would ask Jim, just so he could knock you out. Or rather, I wish you wouldn't. I'd never be able to face Ethel again.

STANLEY: I knew you'd deny it. Anyway, there's no way to know.

NADINE: There is a way to know. Look me in the eyes. Come here, look at me. [Unwillingly, he looks at her.]

NADINE (enunciating clearly): Stanley Rush, you are a weakling and a coward. But Mark is your child. [Looking away.] Mind you, even if I'd had an affair with Jim Masterson, it'd have been no more than you deserved.

STANLEY: Of course you'd say that now. You always were good at acting convincing.

NADINE: As far as that goes, I don't suppose you'd act any differently, either way. It would be against your code of behavior as a Southern Gentleman. For you, the way things are is the good way.

STANLEY: That's true for a lot of people.

NADINE: Not for me.

STANLEY: Anyway, you're right. It wouldn't make any difference. I made my decision years ago to raise Mark as my own.

NADINE (suddenly defiant): I love him enough to make up for you.

STANLEY (shaking his head): Just don't turn him into a mama's boy.

NADINE: I don't suppose you doubt Barbara's paternity?

STANLEY: She looks too much like me.

NADINE: No, you can't afford to doubt. One, maybe. But not two. [Melodramatically] To die without issue, your line wiped from the earth.

STANLEY: Why are you being so cruel?

NADINE: You feel so sorry for yourself. [Implied quoting] I'm the one who made you what you are, I'm the pushy one, your son isn't yours.

STANLEY (giving up; this whole discussion has been fruitless from the start): Maybe I have a right to feel a bit sorry for myself, you know. [Pause.] I do love you, despite everything.

NADINE (silent for a moment): Yes, I know. [Very long pause.]

STANLEY (determined): I'm not going to expand into chemicals.

NADINE (grimly; brought back to reality): I'd like to hear Jim's proposition.

STANLEY: You'll find a way to get around me somehow. You want too badly for us to be rich. For us to travel to New York. To go to Europe. All the things I don't care a pin for.

NADINE: Somebody has to look out for the family.

STANLEY: Nadine, you should have divorced me years ago. We want such different things.

NADINE: I never thought of it for an instant.

STANLEY: Because of the children?

NADINE: Because of you. We were meant to be together, you and I. Me to force you to do what you should do, and you to feel self-righteous about resisting.

STANLEY: That's one way to look at it.

NADINE: Things don't always turn out the way they think they will, you know.

STANLEY: Don't I know it.

[A long silence. The sound of crickets.]

NADINE: You need to check on Barbara when you go in. She asked me to tell you.

STANLEY: Don't you think she's asleep by now?

NADINE: Maybe. She said she had to tell Teddy a story before she could tuck him in. I think she probably finished that long ago.

STANLEY: I love her, you know.

NADINE: She loves you too. Yesterday she wanted to learn how to cook an omelet. She said she was going to marry Daddy and be a good wife to him. [Looking sideways.] If she still wants to when she's old enough I may be willing to let her.

STANLEY: I can't imagine her being that old.

NADINE: The years will go quickly. You'll see.

ACT TWO

1945. First part BARBARA, now 16. She sits at a desk, and is just finishing writing a letter.

Scene One

BARBARA [she writes, saying the phrases out loud as she does so]: Tell that good-looking boy all the way to the left in the photograph you sent us "hello" from me. The one with his cap tilted over his eye. I know it seems I'm being bold, but really I'm just silly. Sometimes sixteen seems ever so old but most of the time not. Besides, I know you won't do it. I'm sorry you can't tell us where you are, but I know that's because of the censorship. Lots and lots of love, your sister, Barbara.

[Flourishes the pen and sits back, proud of her efforts. Holds up the paper, proud of herself, admiring the three sheets she has filled. She seems to get another idea, pulls out the last sheet again and draws a big heart.] There. A heart so he knows I love him. My big brother. [She smiles to herself in happiness. Abruptly she puts the three sheets down on the table, and jumps up, calling] Mother! Mother! I'm done with my letter to Mark. [She listens.] I don't know, maybe a few. [She listens.] But mother, you know I don't like reading over what I've written, mistakes or no mistakes. It's so boring reading about things I already know. [She smiles as if at her own wit, which she doesn't know is indebted to Oscar Wilde, then listens again.] Oh, all right. I'll bring it down in a few minutes. And I'm going to seal it, so don't even ask to read it! That was our bargain, remember! I write it, you don't read it. [She listens.] No, of course I won't say anything scandalous. [She sits down again, humming a tune, makes a face, and ceremoniously turns to the first page. Her reading aloud is interspersed with comments out loud to herself, indicated by < > marks. This is a performance, if only for herself.]

Dear Mark. <So far so good.> [She makes a face, but as she reads she gets involved in her own letter.] Mother says it's been ever so long since I wrote to you, but it's not true. [Taking her pen and underlining each word separately as she repeats] It's not true. It's just that I've been so busy. <Gee, you can say that again.> Of course I love you very very much and you mustn't think that I haven't been thinking of you. [Repeating the phrase as she corrects it] Thinking of you. It is so exciting that you're out on a ship in the middle of the Pacific, fighting the Japanese. I'm not the only girl at school with an older brother in the war, but I'm the only one with a brother in the Pacific. And my brother is the best-looking by far. I know you think I'm silly. I'm not. I'm just trying to be gay so you won't think we're depressed, here back at home. [Hesitating] <How do you spell 'depressed'?> d-e-p-p-r-e-s-s-e-d. No. One s.> [She changes it on the letter, then considers her work for a second.] <That's not right, either. I'll just mess it up a little so he can think I meant it with either one >p' or two. Besides, he never was so good in spelling either. A year of Vanderbilt can't teach you everything.> [She makes another face at the letter, and then begins again.] It looks heavenly there, with the palm trees and the sun. Here it's dreary February, and you know what that means. Mother said to tell you that she'll be writing tonight before she goes to bed, but I'm writing this letter now because she's head over heels in preparations for her dinner party. I won't say she's forced me to write, because it wouldn't be true and it wouldn't be nice. But let's just say she expects me to let you know I love you. She says to send you her love. [She is distracted by something on the wall, perhaps a fly or a moth, and pauses. After a few seconds she forces herself back to the letter. She re-reads a few bits, searching for the spot she's left off.] Preparations for her ... no. Send you her love. Just between you and me, I think she's busy pretty nearly all the time. I mean, between getting so rich and moving into the big house last year and supervising the servants and the Garden Club she goes to and the Flowers of the Confederacy and everything, I don't think she has time to breathe. <Time to breathe.> [She considers it a minute and spells the last word out loud.] <B-r-e-a-t-h.> [She adds an 'e' and says the letter out loud] <e>. I still can't believe we're here. It's such a change from the old house. I know Mother has sent you pictures, but honestly you have to see it to believe it. Compared with the one we grew up in, it's just huge. Has she told you about the library? That's Daddy's, of course, though I don't think he's ever read one of the books in it. He just bought them all at once from the Mortimers, the people who used to live here. Mr. Mortimer died, you know. They're bound in leather. The books I mean. Not Mr. Mortimer. [Giggles.] They smell nice.

There are some naughty ones, too. [She smiles at her own daring.] I know you've heard of them. Like Chaucer and Boccaccio. [She is unsure of the spelling here and begins to spell it out] <B-o-k> [She knows she is going to mess this one up, so she simply says the word again firmly and goes on] Boccaccio. He keeps them on the top shelf, but mother believes in literature, since she was an English major at Bryn Mawr and everything, so I just go in and read them. I think she knows about it, and of course we never talk about those things, but at least she lets me. Sometimes I think Momma and Daddy don't get along so well. I mean, they're kind to each other, but it seems to me that they each live in their own worlds now that there's so much to do at home. Of course with Tyler City Chemicals doing so well Daddy has to be at the office a great deal, even though a large part of the operation has moved to Charlotte with Mr. Masterson. They diversified. <Diversified.> I know that's the word, because Mother explained it to me. Still, I guess I don't really understand what Daddy does all day. I asked Mother once, and she said, he takes care of the administration. I asked Daddy once, and he said, he writes letters. I bet his letters are different than this one! Mother still writes to Mrs. Masterson and talks to her on the phone. You met them once, but I never did. Daddy goes to Charlotte sometimes. Their son Bill is about my age, you know. I don't know if he's good-looking. I think Mother likes having such a big household. Of course she was very wealthy when she was growing up, so it's normal that she should know how to order the servants around. But really her voice gets quite strict at times with cook, whose name is Mrs. Beall. We've had three cooks in a year. I think Mother is hard to please. Or rather, I know she is. Sometimes I think she loves you more than me. We have a new upstairs maid named Bridget. [She spells] B-r-I-g-I-t. <B-r-I-d-g-e-t.> [She considers the possibilities, and then scribbles a bit on the letter.] I've seen Daddy looking at her, and I told Mother and she told me to stop imagining things and mind my own business. That's the last time I'll do anything like that. I even think I've caught Daddy drunk once. I know I'm very naughty to even mention it. I told Mother, and she said, Your father often seeks solace in liquor. [Spelling, proud of herself, as she has gotten it right the first time.] <S-o-w-l-I-s. Solace.> [She considers it, then adds an s] <Two s's.> When we first moved in I to this house I used to like going up to the attic at night to look for the ghost. I don't know if Mother wrote to you that the house is supposed to be haunted, even though it's really not so old. The ghost is supposed to be Mr. Mortimer's sister, who died tragically of love for a soldier in the Great War. I never heard her or saw anything, so I think maybe she's found another house by now. [Giggles.] You have a room too, I know Mother has written you that. Sometimes I go in and sit on the bed there too, just to let you know I'm thinking of you. I mean, it can hardly be your room if you've never been in it, but it's meant to be your room when you get back, when you're not back at college. If you go back to college. Maybe you'll be so old and worldly-wise that you won't need college. Daddy never went to college, of course. He's proud of it, I think. Of course that was then, and now maybe you have to get a degree. Mother believes in college. Mother says I'm going to go to Bryn Mawr, like her. That seems so far away, even though it's only three years. I think things have changed since she went there. She used to tell about the Deans who wore pince-nez and who could freeze you with a stare at twenty paces. [She is impressed with herself, and pronounces it with very nasal and "French" intonation.] <Pince-nez. There.> And the dorm wardens to make sure you were being good and didn't go out when you weren't supposed to. Not that I'm bad, but I wonder sometimes if I'm good. I'm telling you this because I know you'll understand. Somehow brothers do, I think. And even if I haven't seen you in a year I feel we're still close. You never made fun of me like most older brothers. Of course, you're my hero. I guess you know that, so I won't tell you. So big and strong and kind. At school we're studying geography and math and things like that. It's not too interesting, but I suppose I must take an interest. There are things that are ever so much more interesting. I mean boys. There. Am I terrible? Don't worry, you won't have to come and defend my honor or anything. We have dances between Miss Fizpatrick's and the Dewey Day School, with plenty of chaperones, and there's one boy that is so good looking. I nearly died. He danced with me last time. His name is Paul. Paul Swanson. You don't know him, of course, he's ever so much younger than you. At least two years. I impress the boys by telling them I have a brother in the Navy, and show them your picture. I know I'm just going on, but honestly I can't think of anything else to write. I won't let Mother read this letter, of course not with what I've written. That's our deal. I write the letter and I get to seal it. She did read one or two and said they were run-on letters, but maybe you liked them anyway. We pray at dinner every day for you. I am sure Daddy thinks of you a lot even if he doesn't write often. He's not a great writer. I know you think he's a dictatorial old coot. I think he's a sweet man. I hope it's okay that I get along with him and you don't. I think I get along with Daddy and you get along with Mother. That's fair, isn't it? I've run out of things to say. Right now Becky is my best friend but I don't know if you ever met her. Mostly I'm happy. I miss you. Oh yes. Tell that good-looking boy all the way to the left in the photograph you sent us "hello" from me. The one with his cap tilted over his eye. I know I'm being bold, but really I'm just silly. Sometimes sixteen seems terribly old, but most of the time not. Besides, I know you won't do it. I'm sorry you can't tell us where you are, but I know that's because of the censorship. <can't tell us where your ship is, but I know that's because of the censor-ship.> [Looks up, pleased with herself.] I wonder if he'll get the joke? The censor-ship. Maybe I should underline the 'ship' part. Or maybe not. [She considers for a moment, then] Oh, well, maybe. [She underlines and sits back.] Lots and lots of love. Your sister, Barbara.

There. It's fine. [Calls downstairs.] Mother, I'm coming down in a minute. [She gathers her things and leaves the room.]

Scene Two

NADINE (comes in the room in the semi-darkness; turns on the light. She sits at the desk and runs a hand over her hair. She picks up a table clock and looks at it):

Midnight. What a party. I'm exhausted. [She sighs heavily. She sits a minute, then opens a drawer of the desk to take out paper and pen, arranges them on the desk, and sits with them before her. It takes a minute or two for her to begin writing she picks up the pen, lays it down, picks it up again. Finally she writes, and says out loud] Dear Mark. [She hesitates, then begins to cover the paper with lines. What follows is a soliloquy—the one non-"naturalistic" scene in the work.]

My darling Mark, the letter that I am writing you now is only a pale version of what I feel, and what I might think if I allowed myself. I write about what we're doing at home, about the dinner party I've just finished giving, about how well the company is doing, about how we pray for you every night. I know that Barbara will write you her version of some of these things, but because I won't read her letter I don't know how many of them she will talk about. Mine is a newsy letter, a bright, cheerful letter. It's factual; it's loving. I wasn't an English major for nothing, you know. But my letter doesn't say what I would give anything to say, what I would give anything to articulate, even to myself. It doesn't tell what is going through my head as I watch my hand forming the perfect writing, that I learned as a child and have never lost, forming its perfect curlicues across the page. I will finish this letter without having told you what's in my heart, because I never really told myself—at least, not completely, not fully. It wouldn't be good for you to hear it, and it wouldn't be good for me to think it. For your sake and mine I will remain the fond, supportive, but ultimately somewhat distant mother. It's better that way. Better that you not have to bear the brunt of my unhappiness. I didn't want you to go to into danger. But everyone's son was going, and how could I say before others, mine is different, my boy is mine! He must be spared. The words we read about in the newspapers mean nothing to me, words like battles and victories and offensives. The war, they say, is drawing to a close. Germany can't last much longer, Japan must follow. To me it seems that offensives and battles are invented by the newspapers to hide the truth. The only truth is that you must come back to me. Partly my love is selfish. I'm afraid you'll die, and that I will be responsible for your death. It's true, I'm surrounded by wealth. It's my childhood, this wealth, and I love it. I love the richness of brocade in the curtains, I love the heaviness of silver flatware that lies in rows on the table, I love the starched caps of the servants. This is what my father would have had. This is what we would have had. It's my prize, and my penance. Sometimes it seems that I alone am the one who has made these profits in war, I alone am the cause of this great wealth. Not my husband, not even his partner. I made it happen. Without me there would be no corporation, there would be no chemicals, there would be no profits. They are blood profits. They have taken you, my son. You think that you are merely doing your duty, probably you are happy, certainly you have no idea of my anguish. I know that you are brave and have no fear. I have fear enough for both of us; I have fear enough for the whole world. The whole world is fear; the world balanced on the point of a knife blade, your life held in balance while my existence moves forward in its fore-ordained way, my life of a society hostess in the moderate-sized city of Tyler City, in the state of North Carolina. I know that my love for you is too great. No one can bear the burden of such love. That's why what I write to you tonight is a measured letter, a loving letter, but not the letter that I will never write, the letter that I can only imagine. We are like Hänsel and Gretl abandoned in the woods. The birds have eaten our bread crumbs, and now only the wicked witch awaits us. In the fairy tale the brave little Hänsel kills the witch and sets free the enchanted children. But I have often seen this story through the witch's eyes imagine being burned to death in the oven. It was the fate she was reserving for Hänsel, but we do not see it happen to him, and so cannot pity him. I feel the heat on my face, sense the fire, feel my fists beating at the door which burns the skin from my bones as they touch its surface, hear the laughter of the children outside. My daughter seems like a person who suddenly appears in the house, pretending that she lives there. I play along with the charade, because everyone else seems to think it normal. I'm afraid I have done something I can never undo. Save me. Prove me wrong. I feel shame at my selfishness, I feel confusion at the intensity of my love. These are the fillings-in of quivering silences in the real world, that world of ticking clocks and novels and conversations with other people and instructions for the servants. Come home to me and silence the voices, stop up the fissures that open between the reaching out and the taking, the unseen worlds that float between the atoms of the universe. Only you can make me whole again, only your life can still my pain, take away my guilt. [Her hands upraised, her face distorted with pain] Please live, my child.

[The soliloquy is at an end. NADINE picks up the pen again. She talks the last few lines as she writes.] So you can see that we are leading very humdrum lives here. Yours is so much more exciting. I know that Barbara will send her love, so I'll just send [Pause] Love from, Your Father and Mother. [She blots the last sheet, piles the three sheets together and folds them, stuffing them into an envelope.] Heaven knows when he'll get this. The mail takes so long.

ACT THREE

1948. STANLEY's office.

Scene One

STANLEY at his desk, dressed in a three-piece suit. He is leaning forward into a tape recorder, the newest in technology. Dictates.): Dear Lord Carnevallon. Thank you for your letter of 12 June. Thank you as well for your perceptive comments regarding the collaboration between Tyler City Chemical and International Chemicals, United Kingdom, on your upcoming carbon-based research project. Needless to say, we will take your concerns into account. I will be in communication with my partner, Mr. James Masterson, in the Charlotte office, with respect to the matter. We are confident that this partnership will be to the advantage of both of our concerns. Please accept my best wishes. Yours sincerely, etc. [Turns off the machine, leans back. Grouses out loud to himself.] I'll just send a copy of this to Jim and let him take care of it. [Pause.] Window dressing, that's what I am. Sitting on a gold mine and I come in every day and do cross-word puzzles. And write letters. [Speaks into an intercom.] Miss Stevens, I've got a draft of a letter to Lord Carnevallon. No. I'm going out to lunch. You could come in and take it off the machine then. [Listens.]

And oh, Miss Stevens. Send my daughter in right away when she arrives. She's meeting me here. We're going out to lunch. Thank you. [Pushes a button and leans back. Suddenly he is in a better mood. He looks around his office admiringly. Clearly he talks to himself a lot.] Well, maybe it's not too bad for a fellow who started off as a clerk in a fertilizer store. Not bad at all. A big office, that's what I insisted on when Jim and I parted ways. And I've always had it, wherever we've been. Of course, what I do in it all day is a different matter. [Shuffles papers for a moment or two, checks a pocket watch. Looks lost. He reaches into his drawer and pulls out a silver hip flask, from which he takes a drink. Screws the cap on it, and puts it back. The phone rings. He picks it up.] Yes? Good, send her in. [He hangs up. He gets up, ready to greet BARBARA, runs a self-conscious hand through his hair. The door opens and a sophisticated, college-aged BARBARA comes in, a full skirt and high heels.]

Scene Two

BARBARA (holding out her arms): Daddy!

STANLEY (steps forward and hugs her): Right on time! Did you have a good trip?

BARBARA: Yes, and I came straight here.

STANLEY (admiringly): Fancy that, my baby flying all alone. It's better than the train. Faster. We wanted you with us early for Christmas. [Touching her bare arms.] Didn't you freeze?

BARBARA: I left my coat with your secretary. Miss Stevens, isn't that her name? I think I've talked with her on the phone.

STANLEY: She's been with me for several months now.

BARBARA: And I've sent my luggage and all sorts of presents home in a taxi and came straight here. I'm so glad you suggested it. I just had to see your new offices. The company must be doing very well. Everyone at school is very impressed when I tell them my father is President of Tyler City Chemical Corporation. I knew you were important, but I had no idea how very important!

STANLEY: Well, yes. [Pause.] There *is* the main factory complex in Charlotte, of course.

BARBARA: These offices here are so beautiful! And so big! Much bigger than your old ones. This must be where the real work is done, I mean the decision making, not the machinery. And my Daddy the most important of all.

STANLEY (heartfelt): Thank Heaven I have a daughter. [Gives her a hug; then, trivializing as if embarrassed at his outburst] Old men need youth.

BARBARA: You're not old, Daddy. I just came in the lobby and that impressive doorman in the elegant uniform asked me whom I wanted to see—he actually said "Whom do you wish to see, Miss"—"whom," imagine, a doorman!—and I said I was Miss Rush, Mr. Rush's daughter, and he practically fell over himself to direct me to the elevator and then he pushed the elevator button and another equally elegant elevator operator opened the door and delivered me up to this floor, where I found Miss Stevens waiting for me.

STANLEY: You may not be surprised to hear that your mother had a hand in the decoration of the doorman.

BARBARA: Did she? Oh well, trust Mother. Everyone at Bryn Mawr remembers her, you know. Oh, you're Nadine Arthur's daughter? they say, and nod approvingly. She must have made quite an impression.

STANLEY: I was impressed, certainly.

BARBARA (turning around to see): I still can't get over this office. I used to be bowled over by the library at home with all its leather-bound books. But this is ever so much better. [Confidingly.] I used to sneak in and read the dirty ones.

STANLEY: Your mother told me.

BARBARA: Weren't you upset? Fathers always are.

STANLEY: I figured it couldn't hurt you to learn some things through books. Heaven knows I never did.

BARBARA: Yes, I know. The self-made man, and all that.

STANLEY (half to himself): You're still so young. [Teasing her.] Still the same chatterbox.

BARBARA: Daddy! [Looking around the office] I mean, look at all those bookshelves. And the pictures. [Suddenly suspicious.] Did Mother choose the pictures too?

STANLEY: Who else?

BARBARA: She certainly runs the house well, so I don't know why I should be surprised at anything. Next you'll tell me that she's running the business.

STANLEY [pauses]: Your mother has a very shrewd sense of timing.

BARBARA [laughs and plumps down on a chair]: I think it was a fantastic idea for you to suggest we go out for lunch. The whole semester at school they do nothing but make us work work work.

STANLEY: And what has my little girl been working on?

BARBARA: Mostly that Greek history course I told you I was taking this semester.

STANLEY: Yes, I remember. You wrote us. One of your long newsy letters.

BARBARA: You mean one of my run-on letters, as mother calls them. [Abruptly.] Mark took some history too. I found his old college notebooks up in the attic shortly after he died and read them and cried and cried. I know you and Mother still miss him.

STANLEY (changing the subject): Of course, dear.

BARBARA (suddenly covering her face with her hands and then pulling her face up, covered with tears): Oh, Daddy, why did he have to die?

STANLEY: We were in a war.

BARBARA (insisting): Why do bad things happen at all? Like wars? And death?

STANLEY: I don't know what the answer of the Episcopal Church would be, but my own feeling is that somehow things turn out the way they're supposed to turn out.

BARBARA: They turn out for the best, you mean? [Perplexed.] You don't mean that it was good that Mark died?

STANLEY: Sometimes I think that they turn out for the worse. But somehow the way they had to turn out.

BARBARA (excited): I think I know what you believe. It's got a name. It's called determinism We studied it in my philosophy course. It means you believe in cause and effect and free will is just an illusion.

STANLEY (amused, lovingly): Is that what I believe, my dear? I'm so glad my little Bryn Mawr girl can tell me. Sometimes I'm not so sure myself.

BARBARA: Now you're making fun of me.

STANLEY: A little, perhaps.

BARBARA: Just say what you wanted to say.

STANLEY (serious again): I guess it seems to me that whether or not you do the thing you think is the right thing, things will turn out the same way, ultimately.

BARBARA: The same way? You mean, like there's an inevitable end to things? Like Oedipus Rex? You know, the oracle says the Oedipus is supposed to kill his father and marry his mother and he does everything to escape that fate and it turns out to be precisely the attempt to escape that fate that brings him to it.

STANLEY: Wasn't Oedipus a king?

BARBARA (proud of her knowledge): The king of Thebes.

STANLEY: Well then, that doesn't apply to me. I'm not a king.

BARBARA (turning a phrase): Surely a Titan of Industry.

STANLEY: You know I started life working in my father's fertilizer store.

BARBARA: Of course I know, Daddy.

STANLEY: They tore it down last year. It was where the new housing development is now. On the road to Parkerville. That was a dusty country road. Look at it now.

BARBARA (looking around, sweeping with her hand, trying to cheer him up): This is a far cry from a fertilizer store.

STANLEY: And who can say that this is better?

BARBARA: Oh Daddy, you're just being morose. Of course this is better. [Giggles.] Or at least, more fun. [Becoming buoyant again.] Oh come on. You can't tell me that you wouldn't rather be here in this luxurious office in this spanking new building—

STANLEY (interrupting): With the gorgeous doorman.

BARBARA (giggling again): Yes, with the gorgeous doorman. Wouldn't you rather be here in all this splendor than leaning over a dusty counter in a fertilizer store?

STANLEY: Well, that life sure wouldn't support you in pearls. Or at Bryn Mawr either.

BARBARA (flatly): I can't imagine that life. I mean, no more trips to New York! And we couldn't have taken that cruise you and Mother and I took to South America when the War was over. And no more big house! And no more college!

STANLEY: Maybe things would be better if I were still in fertilizer. Mark would still be alive. [Shakes head] I should have loved him more.

BARBARA: But you did love him. I know you did.

STANLEY: I wasn't for expansion, you know. That was Jim Masterson's idea. And your mother's. If it hadn't been for her—

BARBARA: It was a good idea, wasn't it?

STANLEY: When the gods wish to punish someone, they grant his desires. Or hers. Didn't the Greeks believe something like that?

BARBARA: Yes. But how have you been punished?

STANLEY: We got rich from the war. In return, we lost Mark.

BARBARA: Daddy, it was a war. You just got through telling me that.

STANLEY: Isn't there something in the Greeks about family curses?

BARBARA (proud to be able to show off her knowledge): Agamemnon sacrificed his child Iphegenia to insure favorable winds to Troy. And so when he came home from Troy, Clytemnestra killed him in his bath. [Lighter.] I hardly think Mother is going to kill you in your bath. Besides, she was having an affair with another man while he was gone. Clytemnestra, that is. Not Mother. Aegisthis, his name was.

STANLEY: I don't think it's likely that your mother will kill me in the bath. [Pause.] [Treading on dangerous ground] But tell me, did Clytemnestra have a child with this Aegisthis?

BARBARA: No. Or at least, it doesn't appear in Aeschylus. [Getting into her story.] See, she has two children already from her marriage with Agamemnon. The girl is Elektra, and she loves her Daddy. And the boy is named Orestes, and Elektra gets him to kill her mother.

STANLEY: Kill her mother?

BARBARA: For killing her father. It's all very complex.

STANLEY: And then what happens?

BARBARA: Orestes gets chased by the furies, which are harpy-like females, and takes refuge in a shrine. And that's the end.

STANLEY: That's the end? How strange. He doesn't die?

BARBARA: He wasn't personally responsible. And it all has to do with the establishment of law in Athens, and the moving away from personal vendettas, like all the people I've just told you about.

STANLEY: Very little relation to real life, I'd say.

BARBARA: It's not supposed to be real. Besides, it's old.

STANLEY: Didn't you tell me once that the Greeks didn't think much of pride? Going above your station?

BARBARA: It was one of the worst things. Doing things that weren't really the domain of human beings, but of the gods. The idea was that you could do it, but you'd get punished in due time, because the gods wouldn't put up with it. Sometimes the punishment was visited not on the people who had done the bad thing, but on the next generation, or the next.

STANLEY: Of course, we're not Greeks.

BARBARA (suddenly worried): You don't believe that curses work themselves out through families, do you?

STANLEY: If only it would help make sense of things.

BARBARA: Daddy, I've never heard you talk like this before. You *are* depressed today.

STANLEY: I'm getting old, I think.

BARBARA (suddenly suspicious): Have you been drinking? Don't think I don't know that you nip away all the time on hip flasks. I've seen you do it on the sly just when you thought I wasn't looking.

STANLEY (half-amused): Is that so?

BARBARA: You're alone too much.

STANLEY: Sometimes I feel we can be held responsible for things that were unavoidable.

BARBARA: Daddy, I'm worried about you.

STANLEY (patting her hand): Worry about your mother, if you like. She's never gotten over Mark's death.

BARBARA: She has been different since he died. Nothing I do is ever right.

STANLEY: She means well.

BARBARA: Yes. [She has been waiting to say this.] Daddy, would you like help in the business?

STANLEY: Help?

BARBARA: From me.

STANLEY: You help me already by being who you are.

BARBARA: Thank you Daddy, but I mean in the business. I'd like to know more about it. Get involved, you know.

STANLEY [pause]: I had no idea you harbored such ideas. You *are* your mother's daughter, after all.

BARBARA: I've been thinking about it. I'd like to . . . be involved.

STANLEY (putting her off): You know how much I love you.

BARBARA: I know.

STANLEY: I'm surprised, that's all.

BARBARA: Why should you be surprised? You always said I was smart. I could help you. Who knows, maybe take over some day! I'm sorry, Daddy, I didn't mean that.

STANLEY: I know I'm going to die someday.

BARBARA: But not for a long long time. I really didn't mean—

STANLEY: Hush, daughter.

[Silence.]
BARBARA: But what about, well, helping you?
STANLEY: My work load isn't so heavy now.
BARBARA: There has to be something I can do.
STANLEY: You know my feelings about women in business.
BARBARA: All those things are changing.
STANLEY (firmly; cutting off discussion): Maybe in Philadelphia.
BARBARA (sensing implacable opposition): You can think about it.
STANLEY: I've only wanted one thing: to shield you from all the things that men have to do.
BARBARA: But mother was involved with the company. You said so.
STANLEY: That's my point.
BARBARA (perplexed): What nonsense.
[Pause.]
STANLEY: Let's not quarrel.
BARBARA: I could never quarrel with you, Daddy.
STANLEY: I know. [Pause.] Shall we go? We'll be late for lunch.
BARBARA (trying to regain her earlier buoyancy): Lunch with the director of Tyler City Chemicals! How important you make me feel!

ACT FOUR

1950. INSIDE NADINE AND STANLEY'S house. Ostentatious wealth.

Scene One

NADINE is on the phone. By now she is in her late 40s, and considerably more world-weary than in Act One.

NADINE (into telephone): Honestly, Ethel, I wish I knew. She never tells me where she's going. She's so independent. [An artificial laugh, trying to act as if it didn't matter to her.] Since she graduated from Bryn Mawr I hardly see her. [Pause.] Magna cum laude. [She listens.] I don't think she knows what she wants. Right now she's working at Murphy's. [She listens.] She's going through some sort of rebellion, I think. [She listens.] You know his ideas about women in business. [She listens.] I suppose she'll get married, but I have no idea when. Somehow she made it through Bryn Mawr without marrying one of the boys from Yale or Princeton. [She listens.] Yes. Then I met Stanley. [She listens.] But boys are so different. They get their traits from their fathers. Your Bill is so much like Jim, so studious. [She listens.] Don't be ridiculous. I'm sorry Bill and Barbara didn't hit it off. [As an afterthought.] You know how Stanley feels about things. He thinks he's been put out to pasture. [She listens.] Believe me, I tried to get her to be interested. But with you living so far away now it was difficult. And between you and me, my pushing him on her didn't serve as a recommendation. [She listens.] Of course, dear. [Agreeing.] Thank goodness for the telephone. [She listens, then covers the phone and calls offstage] Emily, can you make sure the pot roast isn't burning? [Listens.] All right. [She turns back to the phone]. The new cook. I guess I sound like a fish-wife, screaming that way. [She listens.] Yes, she even offered to pay us rent. On her salary at Murphy's. To show she wasn't anybody's stooge, I suppose. [She listens.] At first I was surprised she didn't go to New York and get a little apartment down in the Village. Maybe she just wanted to plague me. [Pause.] You hear about really strange people down there in the coffee houses nowadays. Long hair and sandals, that sort of thing. [She listens.] Of course she adores Stanley. Only she's mad at him too. I don't know how she's going to resolve that one. [She listens.] For all I know she can be going out with all sorts of boys from town. Sometimes she doesn't get back until late, and when I ask her where she's been, she gets quite snappish. [She listens.] It seems too bad to me, but you know Stanley. He always did say I'd have been better at it than he is. [She listens.] Both of us would have been. But there's no way I could have changed his mind. The more I pushed, the more he dug in his heels. [She listens.] I wouldn't say embittered. Just realistic. [She listens.] You know they fought like two tomcats the year or two before Mark went away to college. Now I think Stanley feels guilty. He and Mark never did get along. And angry at me. He thinks I pushed him into getting rich. In a way I did. He needed somebody to push him. That's why he married me. [Pause.] Maybe we're all just getting old. [She listens.] Of course, I understand. It was good to chat. Yes. Yes. Bye. [She hangs up the phone and looks around, sighing, then reaches forward on the table and rings a bell. She waits a minute, then gets up and walks off, calling] Sarah! [Now talking to herself.] Now where is that girl? First the cook, then the maid. Maybe both of them are drunk in the kitchen.

Scene Two

NADINE, dressed in the same clothes, and STANLEY, now rather portly and dressed in a three-piece dark suit with watch chain, are sitting in two chairs, STANLEY with a newspaper and NADINE with a book. It is later the same evening. There is a carafe of water on the table, with a glass. The only noise is the ticking of the clock. STANLEY turns a newspaper page. NADINE looks up, then down at her book again. She turns a page, then looks up and, as if making a decision, begins to speak.

NADINE: I talked to Ethel today.

STANLEY [looking up from his newspaper]: Oh? How is she?

NADINE: A bit disappointed that Barbara isn't more interested in Bill, I think.

STANLEY: Well, you know my feelings about Jim Masterson.

NADINE (quietly): I think Barbara is disappointed too.

STANLEY: I can't help it. [He goes back to his newspaper.]

[The clock ticks.]

NADINE (re-opening the subject): And there's nothing wrong with Bill Masterson. He's a very nice boy.

STANLEY (looking over his newspaper): A mama's boy, I thought, with his Princeton degree and his overdone politeness. Too young for the war, the story was.

NADINE: He was only a boy at the time.

STANLEY: Well, as far as I'm concerned he's still a boy.

NADINE: I'm worried about Barbara. She's been out all evening.

STANLEY: When she went out in college you didn't even know when she went out.

NADINE: They don't allow that at Bryn Mawr.

STANLEY: Not in your day, maybe. But I bet even you found a way to get around the rules, every once in a while.

NADINE: Once or twice, perhaps.

[The ticking of the clock. STANLEY looks down at his newspaper for a second, and NADINE at her book. She looks up.]

NADINE: I think I hear a car.

STANLEY: Maybe it's Barbara.

[Both listen.]

BARBARA (offstage): Bye! See you tomorrow.

[Both look expectantly at the door. BARBARA comes in. She is in her early 20s. She is wildly happy, throwing her arms around.]

NADINE: You're in a good mood.

BARBARA (going over to her father and kissing him on the forehead, and then to her mother): Hello Daddy. Hello, Mother.

STANLEY and NADINE (each in turn): Hello, dear.

BARBARA (going over to a carafe of water on the table and pouring herself a glass): I'm thirsty.

NADINE (lacking anything else to say): Help yourself.

BARBARA (pours herself some water and downs the glass, then another. She looks around): So what are you two reading? Catching up on current events, Daddy? What's the headline?

STANLEY: President Truman says that in Korea—

BARBARA: Tell me another time.

STANLEY (a bit hurt): Another time there will be another headline.

BARBARA (being silly): Then there's no point in asking for one that will be outdated so fast, is there?

NADINE: You *are* in a good mood.

BARBARA: Daddy, I want to talk to you.

NADINE (semi-rising, as if getting ready to leave): Excuse me.

BARBARA: Oh mother, don't be ridiculous. I didn't mean for you to leave.

NADINE: All right, then. I'll just read my book and make myself inconspicuous.

BARBARA: Can't I talk to Daddy without your getting offended?

NADINE: Of course dear, I'm sorry.

BARBARA (going over to STANLEY and sitting on the arm of his chair): So Daddy, tell me, how's business?

STANLEY (surprised and amused): Never better, dear. You know that. Thanks to my paper-pushing and Mr. Masterson's production of chemicals.

BARBARA: Could you use some new blood?

STANLEY: Anything wrong with the blood that's here already?

BARBARA: It's just a saying, Daddy. You know that.

STANLEY: Whose blood am I supposed to be interested in? I'm not a vampire, you know.

BARBARA (ignoring the joke): Well, a boy's. A man, I mean.

STANLEY: A man?

BARBARA: A real man. [She smiles from ear to ear.] And he even served in the war.

STANLEY: How about if you give me a sense of why I should be particularly interested in this .. what's his name, this he-man warrior?

BARBARA: Martin. His name is Martin.

NADINE (who has been following all this with great interest): Martin what, dear?

BARBARA: Martin Kreuzinger.

STANLEY (sharply): Is he German?

BARBARA: His great-grandparents were, I think.

STANLEY (mollified): Oh.

NADINE (steering the conversation back): That's an interesting name, dear. But as your father was asking, is there a reason why your father should be particularly interested in this . . . Martin Kreuzinger?

BARBARA: Because I'm going to be Mrs. Martin Kreuzinger!

STANLEY (momentarily at a loss, though he should have been expecting this): Good heavens!

NADINE (rising and going over to give BARBARA a kiss, who now is standing up): Congratulations, dear. [Her tone of voice is not overly enthusiastic.] I knew you were up to something. But to tell the truth, I didn't expect this. Well, I did raise you to be self-reliant, I suppose.

STANLEY (stalling for time): My little girl, getting married!

NADINE (more practically): And when were you thinking of becoming Mrs. Martin Kreuzinger?

BARBARA: I wanted to talk to you about that. Martin doesn't approve of big weddings, so I don't think we'll do anything here because it would be all of Daddy's friends and business associates and not really our wedding at all. So we thought, that is to say Martin thought, we'd just get married in New York City next month. Martin has a brother there who's a Presbyterian minister.

NADINE (faintly ironic): Trust you to have definite ideas. And so novel. But let's not talk about the details of the wedding. Things may work out on that. Tell us about our future son-in-law. Is he brave? Handsome? Tall? How will he support you?

BARBARA: He's brave and handsome and tall. And I wouldn't worry about the support part.

STANLEY: He's going to work for Tyler City Chemical Corporation, is that it?

BARBARA (all business): Yes, that's what I'd thought. Of course, he wants to go into politics, but I think he's just saying that because he doesn't know what he wants. How about it?

STANLEY: It depends on what Mr. Kreuzinger is like, of course.

BARBARA: I told you, Daddy, he's perfect.

NADINE: How old is he?

BARBARA: Twenty-nine.

STANLEY (considering): I was twenty-nine when your mother and I got married. What does your Martin do now? And what does he say to this plan to have him work for me? Does he know anything about chemicals?

BARBARA: Did you know anything about chemicals when you took over the business?

STANLEY: I suppose not.

NADINE: What your father means is that we want to know more about Martin. Why don't you have a seat there [pointing to an unused chair] and just start from the beginning?

STANLEY: Maybe that would be a good idea.

BARBARA: I guess this is what's known as the third degree. Where shall I start?

NADINE (encouragingly): Wherever you want.

BARBARA (takes a deep breath): He's the best man in the whole wide world.

NADINE (smiling): How wonderful to hear you say that.

BARBARA: He was in the Navy in the Pacific.

STANLEY (interested): Where?

BARBARA: I don't know, exactly, Daddy. All those places are just names to me. All I know is he was on a carrier, and then didn't get home until the absolutely last batch of sailors, a year or something after everything was all over.

STANLEY: I wonder if he knew Mark?

BARBARA: I already asked him. He thought the question was a little dumb, to tell the truth.

NADINE: Why?

BARBARA: You know, mother, like a New Yorker goes to Chicago, and meets somebody who says, "I know somebody in New York, do you know him?"

NADINE (a little hurt): More often than you think, it turns out the person does know them.

BARBARA: He didn't know Mark.

NADINE: He's not from Tyler City. If he were, we'd know him.

BARBARA: He's from Chicago, but he had an uncle who lived here, so he came here to live with his uncle. He thought his chances were better here than in Chicago. Then the uncle died.

NADINE (mechanically): I'm so sorry to hear that.

STANLEY: What's his line?

BARBARA: He doesn't actually have one. I mean, not a real one. He's been going to night school over at State and working downtown at Johnson's. That's how I met him. At lunchtime I'd sometimes go outside and just sit in the sun and he would too. But I wouldn't call selling suits a line. It's a job, I guess. He's destined for bigger things.

STANLEY (momentarily ignoring this; treading water): So the uncle is dead?

BARBARA: He died last year.

STANLEY (teasing): So your Mr. Kreuzinger thought he'd get a head start in life by marrying the only daughter of the President of Tyler City Chemicals?

BARBARA: Daddy! How could you say such a thing?

STANLEY: What am I supposed to think? The first thing you do is inform me that I'm going to hire him . . .

BARBARA: I didn't inform, I asked. Anyway, he doesn't know anything about that.

STANLEY: You mean he doesn't want to work for us?

NADINE (warning): Dear, didn't you tell me that Jim does most of the hiring nowadays?

STANLEY: I still have enough clout left to get somebody in the door.

BARBARA (as if her mother hadn't interrupted): I didn't say that. I said he doesn't know anything about it.

NADINE: You mean you're figuring out his future for him and not even asking him?

BARBARA: Well, what else is he going to do? It's logical. He's just the sort of man the company wants. [Turning to her father] You'll see.

STANLEY: So far, I admit, he sounds promising. Served in the Navy, working, going to night school. Sounds like he's doing it the hard way, like me. The way every man should.

BARBARA: Oh, Daddy.

STANLEY: But you're not going to tell me he doesn't know you're an heiress.

BARBARA: I don't know whether Martin even knows you have money.

STANLEY: Everybody in Tyler City knows. Everybody elsewhere assumes.

NADINE (trying tactfully to get things back on course): Do you love him, dear?

BARBARA (suddenly radiant again): I'd sacrifice everything for him, do anything for him, starve in a garret for him.

STANLEY: No you wouldn't. No daughter of mine!

NADINE: It's just a figure of speech.

STANLEY: If he's half a man he won't ask her to sacrifice anything for him. He'll work his fingers to the bone to make sure that she wants for nothing.

BARBARA: That's why I want you to give him a job. So he can. I mean, if I can't, he will.

STANLEY (half won over): Well, if you put it that way. [Teasing.] We might be able to find something for him in the stockroom.

BARBARA: Daddy!

STANLEY: What did you have in mind? Vice-President?

BARBARA (now she knows he's teasing): Why not?

NADINE (patiently): Is he a good man?

BARBARA: He loves me!

STANLEY: What do his parents do?

BARBARA (looking over her mother's shoulder): Oh Daddy, I don't know. They live in Chicago. His father runs a store or something. It's all perfectly respectable.

NADINE (in a "there-there" tone): We're both perfectly sure it is, dear. [More practically] We'll have to meet them, of course.

STANLEY (feeling he is losing ground): Are you sure you're going to be happy with this Mr. Kreuzinger?

BARBARA (suddenly determined): Completely sure. [NADINE has gotten up and is wavering between chairs.]

STANLEY (rising suddenly to a statement of credo): Because that's all that counts in life is happiness.

NADINE looks at him, wondering what's next.

STANLEY: You have to be happy with your husband. You have to respect him. If you don't respect him, it'll be hell for both of you.

NADINE: What your father means is, we want you to make the right decision.

STANLEY: It's even more important for a woman. Men have their jobs to throw themselves into when things go badly.

BARBARA: Things won't go badly. I mean, not really.

STANLEY: You have to start out believing that. It's like the steam in the engine that will help you up the hills.

BARBARA: We just won't have any hills, Daddy. That's all there is to that.

NADINE (the practical one): Let's talk about this plan of yours to get married in New York. I'm not saying not to do it, mind, but there are certain advantages to your doing it here, and certain conventions. As the mother of the bride, I feel I need to make clear to you my expectations.

BARBARA: Expectations? What are you talking about, expectations?

NADINE: Well, for one, I had so looked forward to having my girl be married right here in our own church in Tyler City. These things matter to mothers, you know. And your father might be upset if he didn't get to give away the bride.

STANLEY: You're darned right I would.

BARBARA (wavering): Martin doesn't want a big wedding.

STANLEY: Is he ashamed of us?

BARBARA: Don't be ridiculous, Daddy. He just wants to be his own man, that's all.

STANLEY: First you ask me to give him a job, then you say we can't give you a proper wedding.

BARBARA: That's true, I guess. I mean, why not? It's not as if we're trying to hide anything.

STANLEY: I should say not.

NADINE: Then it's settled.

STANLEY (changing tack): What happened to the old days when the suitor approached the father with his heart thumping to ask permission to marry the daughter? At least you were supposed to meet the father.

NADINE (teasing): Your father's code as Southern Gentleman again.

STANLEY (suddenly realizing that this is a can of worms): Of course I couldn't do that with your mother.

NADINE (ironically): Aunt Martha was only too glad to get rid of me.
[There is silence for a moment.]

BARBARA (changing an embarrassing subject): I'm exhausted. Good night all. [Kisses her mother and father, each of whom says "good night." She turns around and smiles at them one last time, then exits.]

STANLEY (musingly): She didn't end up marrying Daddy after all.

NADINE: They never do.

ACT FIVE

One day after Act Four. BARBARA is sitting on a bench at lunchtime, with her brown lunch bag beside her. She is obviously impatient, and keeps looking at her watch, getting up from the bench and looking around, and generally exhibiting all signs of annoyance. MARTIN rushes in. He has been running and his hair is disheveled. He is wearing a suit. He stops short before the bench, looking a bit wild-eyed, and the sight is such that BARBARA forgets her impatience and laughs out loud.

MARTIN: What are you laughing at?

BARBARA: You.

MARTIN: You're not mad I'm late?

BARBARA (playing nonchalant): Mad? I've been sitting in the sun.

MARTIN (suddenly offended, and still breathing hard): I can go away and let you sit.

BARBARA (smiling and pulling him down to her in a kiss): Come here, silly. [She pulls so hard he has to sit down on the bench. When they separate both are smiling.]

MARTIN: I thought I'd never get away. There was an old man in the store who must have tried on ten suits, and he didn't end up buying anything, and it got further and further past twelve and I kept getting more and more abrupt and Mr. Johnson was beginning to look at me funny. I kept looking at the clock, but he wanted me to finish with the old fellow before I went to lunch, and I didn't want to tell him why it was so important that I be here on time, and anyway he wouldn't have cared.

BARBARA (mock-offended, and reacting like her father): Why couldn't you tell him? Are you ashamed of me?

MARTIN: Yes, so ashamed of you that I'm sitting here in broad daylight where anybody can see us, kissing you.

BARBARA: But you're not kissing me.

MARTIN: My mistake. [Leans over, another lengthy embrace.]

BARBARA: I'm convinced. You're not ashamed of me.

MARTIN: Let me know any time I have to convince you again. [They smile at one another, and entwine fingers.] Gosh, it's great to be in love.

BARBARA (singing, to the tune of "London Bridge is Falling Down"): Gosh, it's great to be in love, be in love, be in love, Gosh, it's great to be in love, your fair lady.

MARTIN: I'm the one who has to say you're fair. My fair lady.

BARBARA (being silly): That's what I said. Your fair lady.

MARTIN: Very fair, lady. [He touches her face, tenderly.]

BARBARA (rhapsodically): I feel like a newly washed field on a spring morning. Like a tiny baby rabbit, quivering and wet from its mother. Like a flower that's just bursting from its pod.

MARTIN: Flowers don't have pods. Peas have pods.

BARBARA: What do you know about these things? Some flowers have pods. The ones I feel like, for instance.

MARTIN (suddenly serious): It *is* wonderful, isn't it?

BARBARA: I told Mother and Daddy last night. About us, I mean.

MARTIN (sitting up straight): You did? I thought we were going to wait. Or maybe even just get married in New York and tell them about it afterward.

BARBARA: Well, it wasn't planned. I mean, somehow I just arrived home and saw them both sitting there, and the moment seemed right. They looked so affectionate with one another and I thought, now is the time to tell them. So I told them.

MARTIN: Don't you think you should have waited until I had met at least your father?

BARBARA: That's just what Daddy said.

MARTIN: Did he think I should have asked for your hand in marriage?

BARBARA (laughing): Yes, isn't that a hoot?

MARTIN: I should have.

BARBARA: You're kidding.

MARTIN: Of course I'm not kidding. Maybe not actually ask for your hand, but you know, touch base with the previous generation. Man to man.

BARBARA: Man to man? So this is suddenly a man to man thing? I thought it was a man to woman thing!

MARTIN (not knowing how to explain this one to her): I didn't invent the rules. You have to kind of bond with the father, to avoid . . . any sense of rivalry. I guess there's bound to be some anyway, with the younger man taking away the daughter. But somehow you make it all right by getting his permission.

BARBARA: Rivalry, male on male. Taking away the daughter. I don't much like being the pawn in your game.

MARTIN: I'll have to explain to him.

BARBARA: He wasn't upset.

MARTIN: I bet he was.

BARBARA: I know my father.

MARTIN: You don't understand him as a man.

BARBARA (flailing for a come-back): And do you understand me as a woman?

MARTIN: Of course not. I'm the first one to admit that.

BARBARA (giggles): We're off to a promising start.

MARTIN: What else did you tell them?

BARBARA (suddenly uncertain that she has done the right thing): Well—

MARTIN: Yes?

BARBARA: Of course I told him you were expecting a job in the business.

MARTIN (jumping halfway out of the seat): You told him I was expecting a job? How could you? How could you have done that?

BARBARA: Actually I told them that I was expecting him to give you a job.

MARTIN (now standing and wringing his hands): Tell me you're kidding. That's worse! That's so much worse.

BARBARA: Come on, calm down. All right, I'm kidding.

MARTIN: Thank goodness.

BARBARA: I mean I'm kidding that I told them I expected him to give you a job.

MARTIN (heavily): What *did* you say?

BARBARA: Well, that you would be a very good man for the job.

MARTIN: What job?

BARBARA: As I recall, the choice was narrowed to somewhere between stockroom clerk and vice-president.

MARTIN: Now I know you're kidding. Let's get this straight. I never for an instant thought of working for your father.

BARBARA: I have.

MARTIN: I know you want to work for your father. I mean, I've never thought of me working for your father.

BARBARA: He won't let me have anything to do with the business. I brought it up a couple of times, but it was so clear that he wasn't biting, I finally gave up.

MARTIN: Your father is very traditional.

BARBARA: He claims he's shielding me from sordid reality. But I knew he'd feel differently about a son-in-law. It's a man thing. You know all about that.

MARTIN (stubbornly): I don't know anything about chemicals.

BARBARA: My father didn't know anything about chemicals either. You're like him. You're doing it the hard way.

MARTIN: Stepping into a vice-presidency would be doing it the hard way?

BARBARA: I got the distinct impression that he was leaning more towards the stock room option.

MARTIN: I want to go into politics. You know that. Anyway, I can't accept a job in his business.

BARBARA: I know you want to make it on your own. But you can make a lot more working for my father than going into politics. Besides, what are you going to run for?

MARTIN: Dog catcher. I don't know. I haven't got that far. All I know is, I want to make a difference.

BARBARA: Can you support me in the style to which I am accustomed as dog catcher?

MARTIN: So this is really about money?

BARBARA: You have to admit you'll make more in Tyler City Chemicals than in politics.

MARTIN: Your father will think I'm gold-digging.

BARBARA (impishly): That's what *he* said.

MARTIN: If I have to work for your father to marry you, then I can't marry you.

BARBARA: What do you mean, you can't marry me?

MARTIN: I won't be suspected of gold-digging.

BARBARA: Let me get this straight. You would throw away our chance for financial security simply because my father thinks you might be aware of our financial situation?

MARTIN: I can't believe you're being so mean.

BARBARA: I'm being mean? You're the one who just called off our marriage.

MARTIN (shaking his head): This is a bad dream. I did not call off our marriage.

BARBARA: I start off kidding you and it turns dead serious, with you trying to do some horrible male power play. First you talk about the men shaking hands over the body of the woman—

MARTIN: That isn't what I said.

BARBARA: That was the gist of it.

MARTIN (setting his jaw): I won't have my motives questioned.

BARBARA: Not even by me?

MARTIN: You're not questioning my motives, your father is.

BARBARA (nearly howling): But that's even worse, my father isn't even the one you're going to marry! You'd throw away me because of him!

MARTIN (taking a deep breath): Nobody's talking about throwing away.

BARBARA (breathing hard): Well, what are we talking about?

MARTIN (abruptly): I don't know.

[For a moment there is silence on both sides, punctuated only by the sound of hard breathing.]

BARBARA: Truce?

MARTIN: Okay, truce.

[Again there is silence]

BARBARA: I was kidding, you know.

MARTIN: But you *did* tell your father you wanted me to work for him?

BARBARA: I suppose something like that.

MARTIN: You're putting me in a very difficult position.

BARBARA: I don't see the difficulty. [Relenting] Well, maybe I do. You want to make it on your own. I know that men feel that way. And believe me, women want them to. But under the circumstances—

MARTIN: You want me to sell my ambitions down the river for a guaranteed income. Right?

BARBARA: It's not the money. It's being a part of Taylor City Chemicals. Why not, Martin? What you want to do is so . . . uncertain. I've always said that.

MARTIN (using her weapons against her): And what your father started off doing wasn't uncertain?

BARBARA: That was then, and this is now.

MARTIN: You could have at least waited for him to offer instead of asking.

BARBARA: That's male pride again.

MARTIN: Would you like me better if I didn't have it?

BARBARA: I like you fine just the way you are.

MARTIN: I had no idea you wanted this.

BARBARA: It's so obvious, Martin.

MARTIN: That's what I mean. The son-in-law sponging off the father-in-law.

BARBARA: It won't be sponging. You'll be working hard.

MARTIN: I'm sure of that.

BARBARA: Think of the difference you could make. This is a sure thing. Politics isn't. You have to run. You have to get elected. You have to kiss babies. You wouldn't like that.

MARTIN (growing tender): I'd like kissing our babies.

BARBARA: That's what I mean. We all need to think of our family.

MARTIN (plaintively; his dream fading): I'd wanted to go to law school at night.

BARBARA: Can't you give it a try at Tyler City? If you don't like it, you can always leave.

MARTIN: You wouldn't let me.

BARBARA: Wouldn't let you? What am I, a thug? A bouncer? I'm not 6'2" and 220 pounds! I'm just little old me!

MARTIN: With a formidable power of persuasion.

BARBARA: Have I persuaded you?

MARTIN: Persuasion isn't the word. I don't know.

BARBARA (getting silly, having won): What do you know?

MARTIN (pause): I know I love you. And I don't want to lose you.

BARBARA: You're not going to lose me. I love you. [Pause.] Say you'll think about it.

MARTIN: I'll think about it.

[Silence.]

MARTIN: I couldn't wait to see you today.

BARBARA: And now you're sorry you did?

MARTIN: You have to admit that we've covered a lot of territory. Your announcing the marriage, what my future job is going to be. The only thing we haven't decided on is the name of our first child.

BARBARA: Oh, that's easy. Martin.

MARTIN: What if it's a girl?

BARBARA: It'll be a boy. Just like you. You're my boy.

MARTIN: Another one just like me? Sure you'll be able to stand it?

BARBARA: Silly darling.

MARTIN: It's late.

BARBARA: There's one more thing. I know we had talked about running away to get married.

MARTIN: We never talked about running away. Just about having my brother do it in New York. That's hardly running away.

BARBARA: Mmm. Well, yes. But that's all off now. Mother convinced me that she and Daddy would be heartbroken if we didn't let them give us a wedding in Tyler City.

MARTIN: That's exactly what we didn't want!

BARBARA: I've thought about it. It won't be so bad.

MARTIN: I don't really care what kind of wedding we have. It's for you anyway, really. [Changes tone.] You know, for a girl who said she was going to do exactly what she wanted to do, you're ending up toeing the party line pretty quickly. I mean, a wedding for your mother, and a son-in-law slung over the hood of your car for your father. This is going to take some getting used to.

BARBARA (reasonably): I'm going to get married. Now I see things differently.

MARTIN: Getting married is the same as putting my head in a noose.

BARBARA (not upset): Martin, don't be dreadful.

[Silence.]

MARTIN: Now that you've spilled the beans to your parents, I guess I should meet them.

BARBARA: I forgot. I was supposed to invite you to dinner tonight.

MARTIN: Might as well get it over with. (Looking at his watch.) I have to go. And I haven't even eaten my sandwich.

BARBARA: Eat it now.

MARTIN: I'm not hungry.

BARBARA: I love you.

MARTIN: What time?

BARBARA: Six, mother said. Daddy is going to love you.

MARTIN: What about your mother?

BARBARA: Of course. All women do.

MARTIN: Which includes you, right?

BARBARA: Right. Now run along. You'll be late, and Mr. Johnson will be mad at you again.

MARTIN: I hate selling suits.

BARBARA: It won't be for much longer.

MARTIN: Out of the frying pan and into the fire, I say.

BARBARA: Out of the frying pan and into clover. You'll see.

ACT SIX

1954. The library of the Rush house. STANLEY is leaning over an array of bottles, turned around talking to MARTIN. STANLEY is old and rather bent, MARTIN a young man in the prime of life.

STANLEY: I think I'll have a drink. What about you, my boy? It'll be a while before the womenfolk call us for dinner.

MARTIN: Sure, Dad. Why not? I don't want you to drink alone.

STANLEY: I don't need to hide my secrets from you. You're like a son to me now.

MARTIN: And you seem like a father.

STANLEY: Five years come August, isn't it?

MARTIN (accepting the glass): I really wish you wouldn't drink so much, Dad. You know how it worries Barbara and Mom.

STANLEY: Mother just pretends to be worried. When I'm gone she'll be a rich widow. She's always wanted to be a widow, certainly.

MARTIN: You don't mean that.

STANLEY: I guess it's bad manners to say it even if I do mean it. Now that I'm older it seems to me my manners are getting worse. I say things I mean more often. Not to her, perhaps. But to you, my boy.

MARTIN: Maybe we should all do that. Say what we mean, that is. The world might be a better place.

STANLEY: A more dangerous one, you mean. We used to have a real code of manners here in the South. Don't know what's happened to it.

MARTIN (changing the subject): Sarah tells me you'll be calling on her in the nursery before dinner.

STANLEY: I don't imagine she put it quite that way.

MARTIN: That was the gist of it. She talks well for two.

STANLEY: She's like her mother. Once she starts, she never stops.

MARTIN: Barbara's a busy woman. Haven't you noticed?

STANLEY: I've noticed she's busy. I don't see as much of her. When you come over on Sundays, of course.

MARTIN: Sometimes I wonder where she gets all the energy.

STANLEY: The little one looks just like her.

MARTIN: She was very definite that "Pop-Pop" should come see her before dinner.

STANLEY: I'll go in a few minutes. [Pause. Each sips drink.] My boy, is everything all right with you? You seem so preoccupied.

MARTIN: Why do you ask, Dad? I hope there's been nothing to complain about in my work at the office.

STANLEY: Not at all. I'm proud to have you as my son-in-law.

MARTIN: Thank you, Dad.

STANLEY: I'm counting on living long enough to see you make your mark, you know.

MARTIN (surprised): Well, I should hope so. You'll be around for a good long while.

STANLEY: You get to the point where the years you have left don't seem so numerous any more. Everything is a variation of something that's come before.

MARTIN: I'd say a lot of things have changed. I mean, look at Tyler City Chemicals. Our marriage. Sarah. Not to mention the war. [He hesitates.] Your son being killed.

STANLEY: Things happen that we don't control, that's for sure. I want you and Barbara to be happy.

MARTIN: We are.

[Pause. The door opens and BARBARA comes in. She is more serious than when last seen, and more matronly looking.]

STANLEY: We were just talking about you. Martin was saying how happy you were together.

BARBARA (going to MARTIN and entwining her arm in his): Yes, it's true. Our little family. Sometimes we just sit around in the evening together, I do my club work, Martin reads the papers.

MARTIN: That is, if Sarah is sleeping.

BARBARA: The more she naps during the day, the less she sleeps at night. [Turns to them both.] I've been sent to tell you that dinner will be ready in ten minutes. In case you have to go to the powder room. [She giggles; for a minute it is the old BARBARA.] As mother calls it.

STANLEY: I don't have to powder any part of my body, but I do have a date with your daughter before dinner.

BARBARA: She's silly in love with you, you know.

STANLEY: The feeling is mutual.

MARTIN: Right now she's rather a handful. Definite ideas about everything.

STANLEY: The women in my family always were decisive.

BARBARA (giving him a kiss): Good thing for you! See you.

[STANLEY leaves.]

BARBARA (accusingly): You two were drinking.

MARTIN: Just being social.

BARBARA: I don't think you should encourage him.

MARTIN: It made him feel better to have company.

BARBARA: He's gotten so frail.

MARTIN: He's doing all right.

BARBARA: You men. You think drinking can't kill you. But it's killing him.

MARTIN: Old age is killing him.

BARBARA: My father isn't old.

MARTIN: People age at different speeds. Your father aged quickly.

BARBARA: Have I aged?

MARTIN: I was just telling him how you've mellowed into motherhood.

BARBARA: Do you think that's it? Now that I'm pregnant again I guess I'll mellow some more.

MARTIN (going to her and holding her in his arms): You know how happy I am.

BARBARA: You didn't tell Dad, did you?

MARTIN: You asked me not to.

BARBARA: I don't want to worry them, until it gets a little more advanced.

MARTIN: We were lucky with Sarah.

BARBARA: You don't know how afraid I was when the bleeding started.

MARTIN: Two months flat on your back wasn't fun, I know.

BARBARA: I did catch up on my reading.

MARTIN: You're a sport, sport.

[Pause.]

BARBARA: Do you want a boy this time?

MARTIN: I suppose all men want a boy.

BARBARA: I don't think Dad wanted Mark. At least, they never got along. I guess that's not the same thing.

MARTIN: A little father-son friction is normal at that age. I never got along with my father particularly well either.

BARBARA: What did you and Dad talk about?

MARTIN: He's a perceptive old bird, your father.

BARBARA: Meaning what?

MARTIN: He asked me, rather abruptly, if I was getting along all right.

BARBARA: You are, aren't you?

MARTIN: You know much I hate working for Tyler City Chemicals. I don't tell him. But I can't hide it from you.

BARBARA: I thought that was just adjustment.

MARTIN: Five years is too long to adjust. Your father was rather touching, asking me how I was.

BARBARA: I love to see you two together.

MARTIN: I nearly told him the truth.

BARBARA: The truth?

MARTIN (hesitates, then seriously): Sit down, Barbara.

BARBARA (trying to make light of things): Oh dear, I can tell it's going to be bad news.

[They sit.]

MARTIN: For someone who was so eager to have me get involved, you don't know a lot about Tyler City Chemicals. Not really, that is. Not how it works.

BARBARA: I know that my father is president, soon you'll be a vice-president, and then one day you'll take over as president too.

MARTIN: No.

BARBARA: No?

MARTIN: It's amazing, the change in you since we got married. You forced me into the company, then withdrew from it totally. You never ask me about things there now.

BARBARA: Withdrew? I was never in it enough to withdraw. Anyway, I had my child to think about.

MARTIN: And all your clubs.

BARBARA: I had to keep active in something. Either that or go crazy.

MARTIN: It's a real can of worms, your father's business. I've seen enough now to make your hair curl.

BARBARA (aiming at lightness): My hairdresser does that.

MARTIN (ignoring the attempted joke): Do you even know that the real power in Tyler City Chemicals is Jim Masterson? Your father is a glorified rubber stamp.

BARBARA (getting serious): I'd suspected that, of course.

MARTIN: The vice-presidents don't even report to your father. They report to Jim Masterson. Besides, your father's drinking has gotten to be a joke. They're trying to retire him forcibly.

BARBARA (faintly): Why didn't you tell me?

MARTIN: I didn't want to worry you. Besides, I was supposed to be the competent male, coping with everything.

BARBARA: Aren't you?

MARTIN (ignoring this): Did you know that practically everything we do now is under contract to the Defense Department?

BARBARA: Yes. I'd gathered that much.

MARTIN: Financially, everything is going well. In fact, we're booming.

BARBARA: So what's the problem?

MARTIN: It's rotten.

BARBARA: What's that supposed to mean?

MARTIN: Everyone is on the take. Not your father, perhaps. He's too far out of it to matter.

BARBARA (trying to make light of it all): What do they do? Make personal calls on company time? Swipe the fountain pens?

MARTIN: Kickbacks. Our contractors and sub-contractors pay us to hire them. We pass the costs on to the taxpayers. Once we go into production, if it costs more than we bid on, we simply call it an over-run and bill it to Uncle Sam. The longer I stay the more I see. At Tyler City Chemicals everything is corrupt. That's why it makes so much money.

BARBARA: That's one reason why I wanted you involved.

MARTIN: I'm not going to be involved any more.

BARBARA: You mean: you're quitting?

MARTIN: I'm quitting.

BARBARA (pause; she is trying to think of something to say): Dad will be disappointed.

MARTIN: He knows what's going on. Why do you think he drinks so much?

BARBARA is silent.

MARTIN: Don't be sad. I'd never have become president. There are at least two current vice-presidents who would have stood in my way. And besides, what do you think Bill Masterson is doing in Charlotte? He's the one you should have married if you'd wanted to be the wife of the president of Tyler City Chemicals.

BARBARA: I loved you. That is, I still do.

MARTIN: The time has come for me to do what I said I was going to do five years ago. I've talked it over with the people down at Party Headquarters. They know me. I've helped out when I could, supported the candidates, that sort of thing.

BARBARA: You've been very faithful. And working at Tyler City Chemicals can't have hurt.

MARTIN: They want me to run for city comptroller.

BARBARA (attempt at a joke): Not dog-catcher?

MARTIN (not playing along): Dog-catcher?

BARBARA: That's what you said you'd run for if you went into politics.

MARTIN: One notch above dog-catcher.

BARBARA: Do you have a chance of winning?

MARTIN: They think so.

BARBARA: When is this for?

MARTIN: I've already written my letter of resignation.

BARBARA: I see. [Pause.] Is it really true what you're telling me about the company?

MARTIN: I learned it all the hard way. As it is, I've had to pretend to go along with things in order to keep my job this long. Finally I just got the point where I couldn't pretend any longer.

BARBARA: Do you think Tyler City Chemicals is the only company like that?

MARTIN: I imagine it's a temptation in all businesses. The bigger the business, the greater the temptation. Kickbacks, bribery: it's a way of making things more certain. Raising the odds that things are going to turn out your way. Everybody wants that.

BARBARA: It's certainly a shock hearing about all this just before we have to walk down to dinner with my parents. What will I say to them?

MARTIN: Bad timing, I guess. I had to tell you soon.

BARBARA: It was as good a time as any.

MARTIN: So you're behind me?

BARBARA: My big strong knight in shining armor.

MARTIN: I was ready for tears.

BARBARA (almost a joke): No tears left. I cry nowadays about everything. I guess I'm just exhausted.

MARTIN: Thank goodness little what's-his-name is coming.

BARBARA: His name is Martin.

MARTIN: That's what you said the last time.

BARBARA: This time I know it's a boy. [A spasm across her face. She reaches out to MARTIN.]

MARTIN: What's wrong?

BARBARA: I can't breathe.

MARTIN: Sit down. Here.

BARBARA: I'm in such pain. It feels like last time. The bleeding. God, it's going to get all over my dress.

MARTIN: Just sit. Sit here.

BARBARA: It's worse than last time, Martin. I'm afraid. I'm really afraid.

MARTIN (uncertainly): It's going to be all right. I know it is.

Part Two

ACT SEVEN

1964. BARBARA AND MARTIN. THE DINING ROOM of their house. BARBARA is now the same age her mother in Act One. They have finished dinner.

MARTIN: I wish you hadn't gone to all this trouble.

BARBARA: Didn't you like it?

MARTIN: It was delicious.

BARBARA: Nothing is too good for the Mayor.

MARTIN (patting her hand): I'm not the Mayor until I'm sworn in.

BARBARA: Good-bye intimate suppers for just the two of us.

MARTIN: I'll just resign if that happens. Speaking of just the two of us, where are the children?

BARBARA: Sarah is at Ginny's and Tommy is at Rudy's. I wanted us to have time together before your public takes you over.

MARTIN (decisively): No job is going to come between you and me.

BARBARA: You're finally going to get to make a difference. All on your own.

MARTIN: Even though you once moved heaven and earth to keep me out of politics?

BARBARA: Were they very bad, those years?

MARTIN: It was painful, certainly, watching your father drink himself to death.

BARBARA: I was afraid he would be shattered when you left.

MARTIN: I don't think much of anything touched him by then. He just faded out in an alcoholic haze. Thank goodness he was dead by the time things went really sour.

BARBARA: Well, I don't thank goodness he was dead, but I know what you mean. The Mastersons took most of the hit. The last I heard, Bill Masterson was looking for a job in New York. He was the one I was supposed to have married, remember?

MARTIN: So marrying me wasn't such a bad deal after all.

BARBARA: It was a very good deal. Cheers. [They click glasses.] I feel sorry for mother.

MARTIN: Tyler City Chemicals was her idea to begin with. Hers and Jim Masterson's. She never got over the fact that both your father and Jim Masterson died the same day. The gods cleaning house. Or something. That's what she said, anyway.

BARBARA: Daddy was big on explanations like curses and retributions and divine justice. Maybe she was taking a page from his book.

MARTIN: Do you believe in those things?

BARBARA: It works as well as anything to make sense out of life. [Pause.]

MARTIN: You never liked your mother.

BARBARA: We really should go visit soon. We practically never see her. She's so pitiful, alone in that big house except for the servants.

MARTIN: Maybe we'll invite her here. How about that?

BARBARA: Some time, sure. [Pause.] I don't know if I've ever told you how . . . [searches for the right word] kind you were to stay on at the firm longer than you intended to.

MARTIN: It didn't matter. Not in the long run.

BARBARA: It mattered to me. And I appreciated it. I don't know if I could have stood one more change at that point. It was so horrible for me, losing little Martin.

MARTIN: Who knows who he might have been?

BARBARA: I'm sorry you had to give up that shot at Comptroller.

MARTIN: County Executive two years later wasn't so bad, was it?

BARBARA: Bad? I was so proud of you.

MARTIN: The company didn't take much of a financial beating in the long run, either. Can't keep it down. Like a weed.

BARBARA: A golden weed.

MARTIN: Good for the economy. As Mayor-elect, I appreciate that, of course.

BARBARA: I'm glad we sold off the last of the stock. It just seems bizarre now to think I could have been so attached to a company.

MARTIN: Of course you were attached to it. You were the daughter of the President of Tyler City Chemicals.

BARBARA: I'm delighted you do something different now.

MARTIN: So I have your permission to be Mayor?

BARBARA: You do.

MARTIN (offers wine to BARBARA): More?

BARBARA: No. Yes, all right. Just a little.

[Pause; they drink.]

BARBARA: The children are so proud of you.

MARTIN: Tommy is, anyway. I never know what Sarah thinks these days. It didn't used to be like that.

BARBARA (avoiding the larger issue): Nine-year-old boys love their fathers.

MARTIN: I worry about him.

BARBARA: He's just a slow learner. They're confident he'll catch up.

MARTIN: I guess all parents imagine their children are going to be like themselves.

BARBARA: He's your spit and image, for sure.

MARTIN: And he's one hell of a baseball player. That home run of his last week was unbelievable.

BARBARA: Nobody in my family was ever good at sports.

MARTIN: Your father was too busy, and your grandfather worked too hard. Your paternal grandfather, at any rate. On the maternal side, from what I can gather, you had one who did some hard living while he could.

BARBARA: He certainly left a kind of golden glow for mother.

MARTIN: The people you lose always do. They're not here to wear out their welcome.

BARBARA: Sounds like Proust.

MARTIN: Proust?

BARBARA: The French novelist. He said "The only paradises we have are the paradises we have lost." I remember that from college.

MARTIN: Do you think it's true?

BARBARA: Maybe. To think that I read that as a twenty-year-old. Things like that are too terrible to teach people that young.

MARTIN: It just washes off anyway. Being twenty is its own form of natural protection. You can tell them the worst truths and they think they'll never be affected.

BARBARA: What worst truths?

MARTIN: You know. That people are born plump and unwrinkled and full of sap gradually get saggy and frail and spotty and finally just keel over.

BARBARA: It's called life.

MARTIN: That doesn't make it any easier to take.

BARBARA: Such morbid thoughts!

MARTIN: And how every generation starts thinking it's going to be different from the previous one. The fact is, nobody is different, and every generation makes the same mistakes.

BARBARA (objecting): I'm not my mother.

MARTIN: Sure you are.

BARBARA: That's unkind.

MARTIN: Have you ever thought about how everybody gets a certain amount of pain on his or her plate that has to be eaten? And part of our pain is in not being able to ease others'. Especially the people we love.

BARBARA: I'm sorry you're so down.

MARTIN: Life just wears away at people. We're all victims of spiritual erosion. Didn't you read about that in college too, like Proust?

BARBARA: It's a miracle I remember anything from college. When you become a wife and mother, all the gray cells go into hibernation. Is it like that for men?

MARTIN: We just turn off our brains from 9 to 5 to get through the work day. It saves wear and tear.

BARBARA: Your day is about 6 to 10.

MARTIN: Things will settle down in a month or two. It's just that the campaign has been so hectic.

BARBARA (agreeing): It has been that.

MARTIN: Anyway, how can you talk about your gray cells going into hibernation? You were wonderful with the women voters, and all the speeches. They elected you as much as me, you know.

BARBARA: I appreciate you saying that.

MARTIN: Ask anyone.

BARBARA: I'm my mother's daughter. But I like to think I've put my energy into supporting my husband, not undermining him. [Pause.] Sometimes I think she killed my father.

MARTIN: Good Lord!

BARBARA: My father. Mark. Little Martin. It all just seems too much.

MARTIN: Now things are going to be better.

BARBARA (drying her eyes): I'm tired.

MARTIN: But you still fixed my favorite meal.

BARBARA: Was it good?

MARTIN (patting her hand): Perfection.

BARBARA: And you won't let the Mayor's office come between us?

MARTIN: We really shouldn't talk any more right now. I can see how exhausted you are

BARBARA: We had an election to win.

MARTIN: I think you're wonderful.

BARBARA: You do?

MARTIN: You know I do.

BARBARA: It's just—

MARTIN: Just what?

BARBARA: You're busy all day, and then when you're home you spend what time you have with the children. Sometimes I almost feel jealous.

MARTIN: I guess I thought you could take care of yourself.

BARBARA: I can.

MARTIN: That's what I thought.

BARBARA: But I'd rather you took care of me. I know it doesn't make sense.

MARTIN: That's all right.

BARBARA: Are men always so rational?

MARTIN: Pretty much, I think. Except when they get irrational. And then they fight. Usually each other.

BARBARA: I know what it meant to you to win this election.

MARTIN (expressing self-satisfaction): I'll be the youngest mayor Tyler City ever had.

BARBARA: Not to mention the best-looking.

MARTIN: Is that what you told the League of Women Voters?

BARBARA: I didn't have to tell them. They could see for themselves. I just talked about future and vision.

MARTIN: All of which I fervently believe in.

BARBARA: Whatever you believe in, others will believe in too. You have an aura.

MARTIN (preening a bit): That's what my skipper told me back in the war. That I had something. Maybe he was right.

BARBARA: It's been proven. By the power of the ballot box! [Pause. Takes a sip of wine. She begins collecting dishes.] Here, let me take this out to the kitchen.

MARTIN: Delicious.

BARBARA (smiling): We cooks thrive on praise. Like you politicians.

MARTIN: Hey, lay off politicians. You're married to one. I'm going to be Mayor, you know!

BARBARA: There just might happen to be a chocolate cake waiting for the Mayor-elect.

MARTIN: You're a sweetheart.

BARBARA: Just remember who baked you that chocolate cake when I come to cash in for a favor.

MARTIN: I mean to head a spotlessly clean administration. Unless, of course, you wore a particularly skimpy nightie. [He puts up his hand and caresses her breast; of course she has plates in both hands and cannot resist; she grins].

BARBARA: I'll remember your weak spot, Mr. Mayor.

MARTIN: Even Achilles had one, if I recall.

BARBARA (tone of awe): Very good! You did go to college, didn't you?

MARTIN: Night school, State U. Not Bryn Mawr.

BARBARA: We'll send Sarah to Bryn Mawr. Then it'll all even out.

MARTIN: And Tommy?

BARBARA: We'll figure that out later. Chocolate cake on the way! [She leaves with plates in her hands. MARTIN sits a moment, folds his napkin, pours the last of the wine into his glass, holds the glass up to the light.]

MARTIN (almost whispering): To the future! [He downs it.]

ACT EIGHT

1972. The library of BARBARA and MARTIN's house. MARTIN is sitting at a desk, working on papers. There is a knock at the door.

MARTIN: Come in.
BARBARA (opening door, cheery): It's me.
MARTIN (looks up from his work): Mmm?
BARBARA: Sorry. I know you have work to do.
MARTIN: What is it, dear?
BARBARA: It's Tommy.
MARTIN: Tommy? What about Tommy?
BARBARA: He wants to talk to you.
MARTIN: Talk to me? Why does he need to send you to prepare the way? And why on a Saturday morning when I'm working? Of course I'll be glad to talk to him, but to tell the truth, the timing isn't ideal.
BARBARA: It's hard to find a time when the moment would be ideal. I understand how much time your job requires, but what about the children?
MARTIN: Sarah isn't even around to be neglected. She's going to her peace marches up at Bryn Mawr. And Lord knows what else.
BARBARA: You should be glad that your daughter would act on her convictions.
MARTIN: Convictions, my eye. The twaddle that she's picked up from an unwashed group of long-hairs. Don't tell me that you approve of her politics. She makes no secret of the fact that she uses marijuana, and she supports its legalization. The daughter of the mayor of Tyler City. I'm counting the days. Imagine the headlines in the Sentinel: "Mayor's Daughter Busted For Smoking Grass." What'll you say to defend her then?
BARBARA I'll say that she was going her own way.

MARTIN: You don't approve of what she's doing any more than I do.

BARBARA: I think you're getting middle-aged.

MARTIN (pulling back a bit): I can afford to be middle-aged, can't I, with a daughter in college and a son a year away from high school graduation? At least I'm sure of Tommy. Sarah seems completely unpredictable.

BARBARA: What do you predict for Tommy?

MARTIN (pause): What I mean is, he's a nice boy, and I'm sure he'll do all right. I know you wanted to send him to Vanderbilt, like his Uncle Mark.

BARBARA: I don't think you can have been paying attention lately to Tommy's report cards. Or to him, if you still think of that as an option. He'll be lucky if he graduates, let alone gets into Vanderbilt. That's what he wants to talk to you about. Be nice to him. You can be so gruff.

MARTIN (genuinely surprised): I love the kid. I know he isn't as bright as Sarah, but I don't care.

BARBARA: I know you love him. But I'm not sure he does.

MARTIN: I spent most of the first ten years of his life playing baseball with him. Even after I was mayor I'd take time off to go to his games.

BARBARA: No one was a more devoted father.

MARTIN: So what's this about reassuring him?

BARBARA: It's just in the last few years. You've been busy, and he's been going through puberty. I wonder if you'd noticed.

MARTIN: Of course I'd "noticed."

BARBARA: Remember, he doesn't talk as fast as Sarah. So don't be too overwhelming.

MARTIN: Overwhelming?

BARBARA (ignoring this): I'll go get him. He's in his room. [Raises a warning finger.] Think of how upsetting it must be for him to enter the inner sanctum.

MARTIN: Oh, for heaven's sake. I'll just go up and see him. Or we'll go for a walk together, or something.

BARBARA: This time I think you should let him come see you. He's gotten himself psyched up to do it, and he might explode if he doesn't.

MARTIN: Psyched up? Am I as terrifying as that?

BARBARA: Be nice.

[MARTIN doesn't deign to answer this. Looks down at his papers again. BARBARA leaves the room and shuts the door. MARTIN tries to work a minute, but cannot, finally gives up. A rather tentative knock on the door.]

MARTIN (cheerily): Come in!

TOMMY (enters. Rather hang-dog. In tennis shoes, long hair, poor posture. He stands for a second on the inside of the door): Hi, Dad.

MARTIN (gets up from his desk and goes over to him, fake-heartily): Hello, son. Come on in. I was just doing a little Saturday morning work. Wish I could be like everybody else and take the weekend off. Have a seat. [Motioning him to a chair.] Glad to see you. Your mother said you'd be looking in. [Trying to normalize the situation.] How are things going?

TOMMY: Okay. I mean, fine.

MARTIN: Good, good. Glad to hear it. School going okay?

TOMMY: It's okay.

MARTIN: You doing okay for the Falcons?

TOMMY: Not so hot this year.

MARTIN: Guess I've been a little tied up with work. Not keeping track of things. You still seeing that little girl, what's her name?

TOMMY: Tina.

MARTIN: Tina? I could have sworn she had a different name. You know, the one I saw you with last year downtown that day. It was raining.

TOMMY: Yeah. No, that was Roberta.

MARTIN (false cheery): Tina, Roberta! You've got women coming out of your ears! Chip off the old block!

TOMMY: I like Tina.

MARTIN: Good. What does she do?

TOMMY: Goes to school. Like me.

MARTIN: Want to introduce her to me some time?

TOMMY: Some time, Dad, sure.

MARTIN (a little impatient; he has work to do): So what's on your mind, my boy?

TOMMY: On . . . my mind?

MARTIN (under control once again: patient): Mom said you wanted to have a talk.

TOMMY: Oh yeah.

MARTIN: Want something to drink? We could get Mattie to bring you a lemonade or something.

TOMMY: No thanks. I'm not thirsty.

MARTIN: Well, if you are, just say the word.

TOMMY: Uh, Dad.

MARTIN: Yes, son?

TOMMY: Dad, I just wanted to talk.

MARTIN (encouragingly): That's fine, my boy, just fine. We should talk more often. [Silence.] What would you like to talk about?

TOMMY: Oh, things. I don't know. Like maybe just stuff.

MARTIN: Maybe you're wondering what to do about your military obligation? Are you worried about being drafted? You'll be eighteen next year, and you'll have to register, you know. Unless you want to be like those fellows who burn their draft cards.

TOMMY: They registered.

MARTIN: Hmm?

TOMMY: They registered. What they burn is what they get when they register.

MARTIN (a little hurt at being corrected when he is trying to help): Yes, of course.

TOMMY (finally answering the question): I'm not so worried.

MARTIN: That's good, my boy. I mean, of course it's your patriotic duty to serve. You know I served.

TOMMY: You used to tell me stories about it.

MARTIN: That was a long time ago.

TOMMY: Weren't you afraid of dying?

MARTIN (a bit surprised at the question): Yes. [Unable to pass up the opportunity for a moral.] But you have to do your duty just the same.

TOMMY: If you'd died, you'd never have married Mother, or had Sarah and me, or been mayor. That's weird.

MARTIN: It is a little strange, come to think of it. Of course, there were many families whose sons never got to do any of those things, because they were killed. [Getting sententious.] That's why we speak of families giving their sons. They give up watching the sons do all those things.

TOMMY: You mean I'm here just because you didn't get hit by a bullet.

MARTIN: Well, that's one way of thinking about it. On the other hand, you could say I'm here today because a truck didn't run me over yesterday.

TOMMY: I don't understand.

MARTIN (patiently): I'm just trying to show you that, well, you can't say everything happens because of one particular link in the chain. The whole chain is the whole chain.

TOMMY: So why do things happen?

MARTIN: I don't know. Nobody knows.

TOMMY: Nobody? Not college professors or anything? Not even the Mayor?

MARTIN (hesitating to see if this is ironic; he decides it isn't): I've never heard about anybody who did. Of course, a lot of people think they know. But all they do is disagree with one another, so really there's no point in paying attention to any of them. At least, that's the way it seems to me.

TOMMY (once again abruptly, going back to the earlier point): I'm not afraid of dying.

MARTIN: There's no point in being afraid.

TOMMY: Dad, do you think that each of us has a time? Like, that it's all laid out beforehand?

MARTIN: I don't know.

TOMMY: So if you were meant to have a long life, you could do anything you wanted and couldn't get killed? Wouldn't that be great?

MARTIN: It would be sort of like being Superman, wouldn't it? [Getting serious.] I don't think it works that way.

TOMMY (smiling): I like Tina.

MARTIN (impatiently, feeling that the conversation is getting circular): Good, good.

TOMMY: She likes me.

MARTIN: That's wonderful, son. I would hope she likes you. You're a likeable boy.

TOMMY: Dad, did you . . . have sex before you got married? I mean, not with Mom.

MARTIN: Well son, I . . . [Pause.] yes. Yes I did, son. That's between you and me, now. I don't want your mother to be upset. You know how it is, you're in the Navy, out in the world.

TOMMY: Did Mom?

MARTIN (not following): Did Mom what?

TOMMY: Did Mom have sex before she got married?

MARTIN (trying to answer seriously): When we got married, I thought she was, you know, a virgin. But I don't really know. She wasn't overseas, or anything. Things like that tend to happen away from home. If you mean, did she have sex with me, the answer is no.

TOMMY: Was that because she didn't want to?

MARTIN: I didn't want to. I mean, I wanted to, of course, but back then people had principles.

TOMMY: Do you think it matters if the girl isn't a virgin?

MARTIN: I won't say that virginity in a woman doesn't matter. I know that it doesn't matter in a man. It's generally expected that a man will have a little more experience than the woman.

TOMMY: But who is a man going to get the experience with if not with the woman?

MARTIN (laughing uneasily): That's a good point, son. Other women, is the answer. Women of a different sort. Look, son, I hear you asking me if you should go all the way with your Tina. Is that right?

TOMMY: Sort of.

MARTIN: Have you already gone all the way?

TOMMY: Yeah.

MARTIN (pleased despite himself, trying to keep a stern demeanor): I can't say I'm delighted, but still it's an important day in a young man's life. [Growing expansive.] I say young man, because somehow it makes him a man. You know, welcomes him into the fraternity.

TOMMY: What fraternity? I thought those were at college.

MARTIN: Those are a different sort.

TOMMY: Dad, were you in a fraternity in college?

MARTIN (trying to follow him; it's not his conversation to lead): No son, I went to college a little later than most men, because of the war. I've told you that.

TOMMY: Yeah.

MARTIN: We didn't have fraternities.

TOMMY: Oh.

MARTIN: Nowadays kids go to college at their parents' expense and do whatever they darn well please. Protest. Have orgies. You name it.

TOMMY: Like Sarah? Isn't Sarah doing all those things?

MARTIN: Your mother is a better source for what Sarah is up to than I am.

TOMMY: I don't want to go to college.

MARTIN (he's been warned on this one, so he can't be surprised, but giving it the old "college" try): Don't want to go to college? I think you should see how senior year goes and then decide. I mean, most men nowadays do go to college. Back in your grandfather's day, that's mother's dad, it was different. You could just do it on your own. He did. He built Tyler City Chemicals from the ground up.

TOMMY: I know.

MARTIN: Yes. Well, you don't have to commit yourself now. I think you should leave your options open. You know, just go with the flow a little.

TOMMY: Go with the flow?

MARTIN: Enjoy life. [Confessional.] You know, my boy, if there's one thing I regret, it's not having taken more time to smell the daisies before I settled down. Now it's almost impossible to get the time to do it. [Getting a bit maudlin.] Don't know when I've even had the time to have a simple talk like this one with my son. Even if you and I don't talk a lot any more, you know I still think about you all the time. I mean, you're my son. I love you.

TOMMY (hangdog but sincere): Yeah, dad. I love you too. Dad, I hope ... I hope it's okay that I'm not smart like Sarah.

MARTIN: I don't compare my children. Sarah does what she wants now. You're still my boy.

TOMMY: Yeah.

MARTIN (forced): Remember how we used to kill 'em in Little League? You were some slugger.

TOMMY: Yeah, dad.

MARTIN: You were my boy.

TOMMY: Dad, I have a problem.

MARTIN: What is it, son? Tell me about it. We'll lick it together.

TOMMY: Uh. It's Tina.

MARTIN (leaning forward, leering a bit): What is it, son, she playing hard to get?

TOMMY: No. She likes me. I told you.

MARTIN (sitting back, a shade disappointed): Okay, I'm listening. What's the problem?

TOMMY: I think she's pregnant.

MARTIN (this hadn't occurred to him): She's pregnant? By you?

TOMMY: Huh?

MARTIN: I mean, are you the father?

TOMMY: Yeah.

MARTIN: Father! [Marveling, as if to himself] My son, barely out of Little League, a father. I was thirty when I became a father! Son, how did that happen? Didn't you pull out? Didn't you use a rubber?

TOMMY: Nah, dad. I mean, we thought once wouldn't hurt.

MARTIN: It was the first time?

TOMMY: Nah.

[Pause.]

MARTIN: You're sure you're the father? I mean, She's not some little tramp running around with a dozen other boys?

TOMMY: Dad! I told you, she likes me.

MARTIN sits silent.

TOMMY: Uh Dad.

MARTIN: Yes, son?

TOMMY: You're not going to get mad at me, are you Dad? I mean, I'm sorry and all. I know I shouldn't have.

MARTIN (his mind already beyond the problem to the solution, a bit distractedly): It's okay, son. [Focusing] Son, do you want to marry this girl?

TOMMY: Marry?

MARTIN: Yes! Marry her. I mean, you're only sixteen, almost seventeen, but . . .

TOMMY (with great certainty): I don't want to get married.

MARTIN (this brings him back to reality): No, of course not. What am I thinking? You're far too young. And you came to me to give you a solution to your problem. All right, son. I'll solve your problem. It's not a big deal, as you would say. I don't want you to worry about a thing. I know a doctor, we'll get this Tina to go to him. The doctor will help her, and she'll be all right.

TOMMY: You mean, get her to have an abortion?

MARTIN (the word has sealed the man-to-man bond): Yes, an abortion. That's clearly the best thing. Don't you think?

TOMMY: Well gee Dad, I mean, I don't know.

MARTIN: You came to me to have this problem solved and I'm solving it for you. You don't want to marry the girl, and you're not sure about an abortion. What's the alternative?

TOMMY: I thought— [trails off].

MARTIN (controlling himself): Son, you tell me in your own words, and at your own speed, what it was you thought would happen.

TOMMY: I wasn't sure. I mean, I didn't know.

MARTIN (a bit like catechizing an idiot): Tell me what you thought might happen.

TOMMY (hesitates): Well dad, you know I thought maybe you and mom might—

MARTIN: Might what?

TOMMY (hanging his head): Might take the baby.

MARTIN (losing control for a moment despite himself): You thought I might take your bastard child? And raise it?

TOMMY: What if it's a boy? It might be better than me. It might make up for . . . me.

MARTIN (getting up and hugging him): There's nothing to make up for.

TOMMY (tearful): Oh Dad.

MARTIN: You thought I'd be mad at your losing your virginity and glad that your girl was going to have a baby? What a crazy kid you are. A young man. A crazy young man. [This last affectionately, the father holding the son by the nape of his neck. The clinch is short. Once again hearty.] But hey. [Gives his son a fake boxing jab.] You've gotten this girl in trouble and we're going to do something about it. It won't be the first time something like this has happened to a guy like you. Like I say, we'll just get her to go to this doctor friend of mine, strictly on the Q.T., you know. Don't say a word to your mother. Tell Tina not to say a word to her mother. I mean, even if it's not yours, we don't want Tina to be in the soup, do we? [As if suddenly occurring to him] Does she want the child?

TOMMY: I don't think so, Dad. She's scared. That about you taking it, well, that was my idea. I guess it was kind of dumb. I mean, having a brother or sister that was my baby.

MARTIN (dryly): There's no denying that the situation would be awkward. No, I don't fancy becoming a father again at my age. [Trying to establish a bond] Changing all those diapers, you know. Once through is enough. And you need to be concentrating on your studies.

TOMMY: Oh, Dad, I will, now. I mean, I've been scared shitless. I mean, I've been real scared. I didn't know what was going to happen. I didn't dare come talk to you.

MARTIN: Nonsense, my boy. You come talk to me any time you want. This is not a big problem. It's normal, you know. Part of growing up. Part of becoming a man.

TOMMY: Dad, it feels almost like old times. Like when you came out to see me in Little League. Those were the best times. I would always try to hit a home run for you. Just for you. I wish I could hit a home run for you now. So you'd be proud of me.

MARTIN: I am proud of you, son. I'm proud of you for being you.

TOMMY: It seems like all I do is screw up. I'm not so good at school. Even baseball isn't so great any more. I was afraid to come to you. I was afraid you'd be disappointed. And then the stuff last year. And then this with Tina.

MARTIN: The stuff last year?

TOMMY (not hearing the tone of voice): You know, Dad. When Mom came to the station. She said you had decided that I'd learned my lesson.

MARTIN (of course he has no inkling of this): Oh, yes, that. Yes, your mother and I talked about it.

TOMMY: I know you liked Sarah better than me. But now that she's kind of wild at college, well, I thought it was my chance again.

MARTIN: I love you both.

TOMMY (insisting, making the strongest case against himself): But you have to admit that you were big on Sarah. First in her class, homecoming queen. You name it. I'm not even good-looking the way Sarah's good-looking.

MARTIN: Men don't have to be good-looking. And you're a fine-looking boy. Of course, if you'd cut your hair, and stand up a little straighter. . . [realizing that now is not the time for a lecture]. But that's minor. [Suddenly rhapsodic] My boy, the future stands before you. Who knows what you won't accomplish? You're just a slow starter. Some of the greatest things ever accomplished were done by slow starters. You don't have to go to college, if you don't want to. You can become, I don't know, become a U.S. Marine and become a war hero. You can work your way up in a company. Not Tyler City Chemicals, of course. But somewhere. The possibilities are endless!

TOMMY: I have to go.

MARTIN (doesn't want this fragile bond to be ruptured so soon): Go?

TOMMY (getting up): Yeah, I told Tina I'd meet her at 11.

MARTIN: You remember to tell her what I told you. We'll solve your little problem, and in a month's time neither of you will know why you worried.

TOMMY (gratefully): Thanks, dad. I mean, thanks. [Already at the door.] I'll . . . I'll try to hit you a home run.

MARTIN is left alone. He hits his hands together and begins to pace.]

ACT NINE

1975. The den in MARTIN and BARBARA's house. It is almost completely dark. MARTIN is sitting in an arm chair, staring ahead into the darkness. He shifts a bit, but the scene opens with a long period of nothing happening, MARTIN staring ahead. Finally, we hear faint sounds of someone coming in; BARBARA enters.

BARBARA: It's so dark in here. [She fumbles forward and makes her way to a lamp, which she turns on. She straightens up, turns around, and is startled to see MARTIN sitting there. He looks up at her, but does not speak.]
BARBARA: What are you doing sitting in the dark?
MARTIN (a bit tonelessly): Just resting.
BARBARA (despite the flood of words, the effect here should not be that of an air-head. This is not chatter, it is simply practiced conversation of a public woman good at filling up space that is left to her. The speed is not breakneck, it's just that he isn't responding, so the machinery continues to grind): Well, for heaven's sake. You might have left a light on. [Beginning to fuss a bit, and to get up speed again.] What a mess downtown. I can't remember when we had snow last. Of course, there was that sprinkle last year, but that was hardly more than a dusting. People were running around like crazy folks. At Bryn Mawr, we thought we were lucky to see a winter without four or five major storms. It wasn't winter without snow. I so enjoyed going up to see Sarah at Christmastime when she was there. It really brought back old times. I don't think Sarah much liked the snow, though. She should be coming in any minute, you know. The drive from Chapel Hill isn't very long, and she said she'd be home this weekend. I'll be so glad when she's done with law school. I think she was glad to be back down South. And I'm glad that she's settled down. No more protesting. Well, the war's over. I think she's become more responsible. Maybe it's law school that did it for her. Three years aren't so long. For us, anyway. For the children, I know they seem endless. She said she'd stop and pick up Tommy on the way too. It's so difficult for bartenders to get a Friday night off. But he said he wanted to see her, and us, and he managed to do overtime or something. Anyway they'll be here in a while. I expect them before dinner. I'll have to go and shake up Hazel. She's not quite as

energetic as she used to be. [Slight pause.] How was the Mayor's day? Any more on the nomination? I don't think it's any too early for them to get you committed. Once they do, there's no question who'll be the next Governor. I don't know that I'll want to move to Raleigh, but sacrifices, sacrifices! [Looks at him.] But dear, I'm sorry. I'm talking a blue streak. I guess it's because I'm excited about nomination, and the Auction. I'll be glad when it's over. But if I do say so myself, I really am the best person to chair it, aside from being Madame Mayor. Everyone agrees. I think we make a good team. [MARTIN looks up at her, stirs, but says nothing. She is concerned.] Dear, what's wrong?

MARTIN: Why don't you sit down, Barbara? Have a drink, and get me one too while you're at it.

BARBARA (relieved to hear him talking): I can hardly sit down if I'm supposed to get you a drink, can I? [Goes over to him and pecks him on the forehead.] I'll do first one and then the other. [Some of her irony returns. The last years have been hard on the nuances, but she has not been left completely without reserves.] I bet none of your staffers fixes you your scotch-on-the- rocks like me.

MARTIN (smiling a shade): No, there's something in the way you combine the ingredients.

BARBARA (goes over to the sideboard and fixes two drinks. As she does so, she talks.): The one who should be fixing you the drink is Tommy. We've never gone to his bar. I mean, of course it's really too far away, but he likes living there. Frankly, I think it was upsetting for him to live in the city where his father is mayor. He feels that he's failed somehow, the poor boy. Not going to college, of course, and not being up to Sarah's intellect. It was clear from the first that she was the smart one. Here you are. [Hands him his drink.]

MARTIN: Thank you. [She sits down, opposite him.]

BARBARA: Cheers. [They clink glasses.] It's been a long time since you beat me home. Did you decide to take the Friday afternoon off?

MARTIN: Not exactly.

BARBARA: I know you never take time off. You're the hardest working mayor this city has ever had. I can attest to that.

MARTIN: Barbara—

BARBARA (hastily): I decided years ago that I was willing to sacrifice you to the good of the people. It was hard at first, of course.

MARTIN: Barbara—

BARBARA: Of course, both of us are pretty nearly worn out after the long day. But I guess that comes with the territory. We knew it would be like this when you got into it. Maybe not exactly how it would be, but the basic lay of the land. You know, the long hours and all that.

MARTIN (suddenly): Barbara, could you please shut up?

BARBARA (very hurt indeed): Well, if you put it that way.

[Pause.]

MARTIN: We need to talk.

BARBARA: It seems to me that I've been doing nothing but talking. But you mean you and me together. A conversation.

MARTIN: I suppose I mean me. Me talk.

BARBARA: I'm eager to hear about your day, or whatever it is that you want to talk about.

MARTIN: Barbara, have you seen the paper today? Or listened to the news?

BARBARA: I've hardly had time to sit down, much less pay attention to the latest scandals and robberies. Why?

MARTIN: Take a look at the paper now.

BARBARA (trying for levity): Before I finish my drink?

MARTIN: Yes, please. [He reaches forward and hands her the paper that he has had on his lap.]

BARBARA: I think it's nice that you want to talk seriously about the news. [Afraid she has hurt his feelings.] I didn't mean to criticize. It's just that you're so busy.

MARTIN: Busy—

BARBARA: What do you want me to read? [Perusing newspaper, she has gotten it from the bottom.] Snow Lames City. Well, that's what I was telling you about. I don't have to read an article about that. Auction Set For Hospital. I certainly don't have to read about that. I mean, I'm in it. Unless that's what you wanted me to see? You're sweet, but there are so many articles like this, dear. Mayor Indicted ... [stopping, then resuming] in Tyler City Chemical Influence Peddling Probe. Oh my God. [She is silent a moment while she reads.]

MARTIN: I'm tired of lying. And you can't testify against me.

BARBARA (suddenly grim): Maybe you'd better just talk.

MARTIN: Money, Barbara. Kickbacks.

BARBARA: From Tyler City Chemicals?

MARTIN: Yes.

BARBARA: But you don't even have anything to do with them. Not any more, I mean.

MARTIN: They came to me. I didn't come to them. If it matters.

BARBARA (silent, then): You involved in bribery? Mr Squeaky-Clean, who resigned from Tyler City Chemicals because it was corrupt?

MARTIN: Ironic, isn't it?

BARBARA: You can't be the same man I married.

MARTIN: I'm not.

BARBARA: You had principles!

MARTIN: Principles erode.

BARBARA: We have enough money.

MARTIN: I had expenses.

BARBARA: I still have some from Daddy. Why didn't you ask me for it?

MARTIN (grimly humorous): To give to another woman?

BARBARA (long pause): Another woman?

MARTIN: Tawdry, isn't it? Well, you'll know soon enough.

BARBARA: That's nonsense. You aren't having an affair. I'd have known.

MARTIN: Come on, Barbara. How close were we, after all? You had your job, I had mine.

BARBARA: My job was your job.

MARTIN: Try to understand, Barbara.

BARBARA: Understand?

MARTIN: Please.

BARBARA (gives in): I'm listening. I don't know who I'm listening to, but I'm listening. Certainly not the man I married.

MARTIN: That was a long time ago.

[Pause.]

BARBARA: Keep talking.

MARTIN: I'm in love.

BARBARA (grim, ironic): Not, I gather, with me?

MARTIN: If it's any consolation, I was once.

BARBARA: Who is it?

MARTIN: Nobody you know.

BARBARA (grim): But I'm going to know her, right? Along with all your devoted supporters in Tyler City?

MARTIN (a bit wearily): My hope, at any rate, is that she'll be spared all that.

BARBARA: But I won't. Be spared, I mean.

MARTIN: I'm afraid not.

BARBARA (wearily): Who is she?

MARTIN: Her name is Miss Saunders. Rebecca Saunders. She lives in Petersburg.

BARBARA: And she's your . . . expenses?

MARTIN: Hotels, an apartment. Jewelry.

BARBARA: You ruined yourself and betrayed me to buy jewelry for your mistress?

MARTIN: Mistress such an old-fashioned term.

BARBARA: Your whore!

MARTIN: Say: my friend. My love.

BARBARA: Oh my God.

MARTIN: I knew you wouldn't understand.

BARBARA (ironic): I understand. She's younger than I am.

MARTIN: As a matter of fact, yes.

BARBARA: Just how old is she?

MARTIN (grimly amused): About Sarah's age. A little older.

BARBARA: Oh my God.

MARTIN: You really are going to have to stop saying that.

BARBARA (infuriated): Don't you dare tell me what I am going to have to say or not say!

MARTIN: Shall I just shut up?

BARBARA (anger making her descend to country music clichés): No! I want to hear the awful truth from your own lying lips!

MARTIN (faintly ironic): My lying lips.

BARBARA: Of course she's got a flatter stomach than I do. She hasn't had two children. Two children and a miscarriage. Oh my God, to think that I thought of that child as another you. I wish you'd died before you were born like little Martin.

MARTIN (wearily; they've been through this): We don't even know the child was a boy.

BARBARA: To me he was a boy. And don't you dare try to change the subject. Just answer me, is her stomach flat or is it not?

MARTIN (raising his hands to an unseen God): Dear Lord, save me. Her marriage is breaking up, her husband is in disgrace, and all she can think about is a flat stomach.

BARBARA: Lord, kill all lying men who steal a lifetime from a woman and then throw her away when a younger one comes along.

MARTIN: I'm waiting for the thunderbolt.

BARBARA: How can you joke at a time like this?

MARTIN: What else is there left to do? You were asking about my relations with Miss Saunders, and I'm prepared to tell you.

BARBARA: "Miss Saunders." Whore!

MARTIN (ironic; he has momentarily the upper hand): Watch the language.

BARBARA: I think you're enjoying this.

MARTIN: Miss Saunders's stomach is flat. She has great tits too. She's firm, and young. And I made love to her until she begged for mercy! *She thinks I'm sexy.*

BARBARA (who can't believe she is hearing this): Martin—

MARTIN (decisively): I love her, Barbara. She's full of life, she wants me. She loves me.

BARBARA (far away): I loved you too.

MARTIN: I'd do anything for her.

BARBARA: You already have.

MARTIN: She'll stick with me through thick and thin.

BARBARA: You poor ninny. She's clearly a gold-digger.

MARTIN: Your insults can't hurt her.

BARBARA (screaming, losing it): She's a slut, this Miss Tits. You dumb ox. What about the jewelry?

MARTIN (distant, smiling faintly): Tokens of my affection.

BARBARA: You can't have thought you'd get away with it.

MARTIN (sincere again): I love her. It's paradise, Barbara, you have no idea.

BARBARA (dryly): Are you referring merely to sex, or to less transient pleasures?

MARTIN: To it all. [Insisting] I love this woman.

BARBARA: The most common story of all. Common in both senses. Man goes through middle-aged virility crisis and picks up a little tart. What's not so common is the fact that you've managed to disgrace not only yourself, but the whole city at the same time.

MARTIN: I'm only too aware of that.

BARBARA: I don't think you have any idea of how ridiculous you are, with your tongue hanging out of your mouth, and your [hesitates a split-second] dick hanging out of your pants. Running after some slut who was taking you for all she could get from you.

MARTIN (defiant): We'll just see.

BARBARA: Do you think Miss Tits is going to be waiting at the prison door when you get out?

MARTIN: Miss Saunders. Her name is Miss Saunders. And I don't think I'm going to prison. Remember how smart a lawyer Johnson is.

BARBARA: Arthur Johnson? I can't believe this. This isn't bad melodrama, this is farce. The same lawyer who got off Bill Masterson . . . how long ago was it?

MARTIN: Just yesterday.

BARBARA: Do you think you're going to get off?

MARTIN: Stress and instability. Besides, with me resigning, the air will be out of the balloon. They may not even prosecute.

BARBARA (one last attempt; hopefully): You're not kidding about any of this, are you?

MARTIN (formally): I plan to marry Miss Saunders.

BARBARA: "Disgraced Ex-Mayor of Tyler City to Marry Whore." I'll look forward to reading the headlines on that one too.

MARTIN (changing tack): I don't think you realize how intolerable our marriage had become.

BARBARA: Now I'm supposed to feel sorry for you? In a minute it'll all be because his wife didn't understand him.

MARTIN: That's right. His wife didn't understand him.

BARBARA: Who could have? It seems there were depths that no one could have plumbed. I just don't understand how you could have met this woman without my knowing. Without my even suspecting.

MARTIN: A few business trips here and there, some long lunchtimes. The usual.

BARBARA: You wanted to go into politics to do good, as I recall.

MARTIN: I didn't expect you to understand.

BARBARA: How right you were. And I doubt if the law will understand either.

MARTIN (plaintively): You have no idea how hard it is being in the public eye all the time. Twenty-four hours a day. You begin to feel like a shadow, an image on the television screen.

BARBARA: In short, a politician. Which, as I recall, is exactly what you wanted to be.

MARTIN (earnestly): I knew I'd have to please other people, but I had no idea that I'd become other people. I was nothing but a string of words, of campaign promises, of empty smiles and insincere handshakes.

BARBARA: I'm almost weeping.

MARTIN: Then you deserted me.

BARBARA: Deserted you? I did everything for you. I campaigned. I cut ribbons. I made speeches.

MARTIN: That was your outside self. Your inside self was somewhere else. Gone. Dead.

BARBARA: Do you honestly think you can blame this on me?

MARTIN: Who knows, perhaps our two former selves are wandering somewhere, far from our turmoil down below, holding hands in a field of buttercups. The two people who got married twenty-five years ago.

BARBARA: You poor pitiable man. Not contemptuous. Pitiable. Beyond pity. Ridiculous.

MARTIN: Am I ridiculous, dear? I suppose I am.

BARBARA: I'm not so worried about Sarah. But Tommy still idolizes you.

MARTIN: I'll tell them that my enemies are out to get me and that you and I have decided to split up. He'll believe me. Sarah is a different story.

BARBARA: Yes, Sarah is a different story. We'll see what she has to say.

MARTIN: We *have* decided to split up, haven't we?

BARBARA: If you mean, do I refuse to spend another night under the same roof with you, the answer is yes. Which means you're free to go to your whore.

MARTIN: When this is over she'll be Mrs. Kreuzinger.

BARBARA: Will she wear her jewels to the wedding?

MARTIN: I imagine so. Not that there *are* so many. Money doesn't go very far at the jewelry store. The rest is already gone. On good times, you know. [Reflectively] I think she thought I was rich. And then, she had no idea of the price tags.

BARBARA: No idea my foot. She knew exactly what things cost.

MARTIN (simply, and if possible convincingly): She liked beautiful things and a good time. It gave me pleasure to give them to her. One thing led to another, and finally it didn't matter. All that mattered was the way she looked at me. It was meant to be.

BARBARA: You were meant to be governor! That was meant to be! This is a perversion!

MARTIN: Obviously I wasn't very happy being mayor. How could I have kept up the charade as governor?

BARBARA: You're a hollow man.

MARTIN: Yes. And the only person who fills the hollow is Becky.

BARBARA (pause): Then you must go to her. If she'll have you.

MARTIN: She'll have me.

BARBARA: The children are coming. I hear the car.

MARTIN: Tell them whatever you like.

[Silence. Faintly, the sound of a car door slamming. Two voices "We're here." The sound of steps, voices. MARTIN and BARBARA are on their feet, facing the door.]

MARTIN: Help me out, dear. One last time. Put on that smile that you do so well. I'll deny the charges. And tell them we've decided to separate. Let them think this is something we've talked over.

BARBARA: How dare you?

MARTIN: Please, Barbara. For old time's sake. Give me that.

[The door opens and SARAH and TOMMY, ages 22 and 19, burst in the door.] Both Hi Mom! Hi Dad!

MARTIN (sotto voce; one last appeal): Help me.

BARBARA (moment of hesitation, she looks at him, then kicks into gear as the old BARBARA she is going to paper it over, insofar as she can): Dears! How lovely to see you!

ACT TEN

1980. SARAH and MARTIN are sitting on a park bench not unlike that in Act One. MARTIN is wearing more casual clothing than before; SARAH is dressed like the professional woman she is.

MARTIN: Such a beautiful spring day. Crocuses everywhere, birds. Reminds me of Chicago. Of course, winters in Chicago are much worse than they are here. Months of snow. When spring finally came and the winds stopped blowing in over the lake, and the plants began to grow in the parks, and in the cracks between the sidewalks, it really felt like a rebirth. A starting over again.

SARAH: Would you like to start over again?

MARTIN: You can't turn the clock back. There's no point in thinking that if you had it all to do over again you'd do anything different. People being what they are. Me being who I am.

SARAH: I'm glad we were able to meet.

MARTIN: The life of a premature retiree isn't full. Your mother gives me my allowance on the condition that I don't come near her. I think Tommy hates me.

SARAH: He has his own problems with Sondra and Billy.

MARTIN: Do you think he and Sondra will get married some day?

SARAH: I don't know. People have children nowadays without getting married.

MARTIN: I worry about how he can support them on a construction worker's pay. As far as that went, bartending was better.

SARAH: He wasn't very good at it.

MARTIN: I thought he was fine, that one time I went to see him. Shortly after . . . you know. After my resignation. It wasn't a good visit.

SARAH: He didn't know how to deal with it. He idolized you.

MARTIN: How *did* you deal with it?

SARAH: Our relation was a bit more distant to begin with, yours and mine. In later years, anyway.

MARTIN: And you'd seen more of the world.

SARAH: You certainly didn't approve of what I was up to back then, did you Dad? Between the protests and the pot, I mean.

MARTIN (mildly): I have to admit that they seemed wrong to me.

SARAH: And now?

MARTIN: I've learned to be less absolute, I suppose. The world is a strange place.

SARAH: I know. [Changing the subject.] I went to see Becky, you know.

MARTIN (very surprised): You saw Becky? Recently?

SARAH: Fairly recently. I was in Petersburg on business, and I looked her up. She lives in a little apartment there. She works as a secretary. An Administrative Assistant, as they call them nowadays.

MARTIN: That was kind of you.

SARAH: I think she was kind to you. There you were with mother and us two the day you resigned, smiling at the cameras and denying that there had been any wrongdoing, and denying the existence of any other woman. Her existence. And she was still willing to see you when it was over. Not to marry you, of course. That was just your idea.

MARTIN: I really thought it was a new beginning.

SARAH: Do you regret leaving Mother?

MARTIN: I guess Becky wasn't the woman I thought she was.

SARAH: Women like that never are.

MARTIN: "Women like that."

SARAH: I feel sorry for Becky. She's bright, you know.

MARTIN: Do you think so? I'm glad.

SARAH: And lonely. I think I can see things from her point of view. A young woman is flattered by the attentions of an important older man. The psychologists would tell you that the woman is trying to marry the father.

MARTIN (wincing): Ouch.

SARAH: But you *are* old enough to be her father. No sense denying that.

MARTIN: I'm not trying to deny it. Just to forget it.

SARAH: She told me that she loved you. Had loved you, rather.

MARTIN (triumphantly): I knew it. I told your mother so, and she said it was just the money.

SARAH: There was that too, of course. She had nothing, no parents, no job. She was very young. You showered her with things. How was she to resist?

MARTIN: You make it sound as if I seduced her.

SARAH: What's your version? She threw herself at you?

MARTIN: As a matter of fact, yes.

SARAH: That's the way it seemed to you. But what was she throwing herself at? A lonely middle-aged man who wasn't getting along with his wife? The Mayor of Tyler City? Someone who gave her entrance into a world she had only dreamed of? People are just the tip of an iceberg in their situations. There's no such thing as individuals loving individuals, it's a situation that loves a situation.

MARTIN: You make it sound so dry. Is this what comes of graduating at the top of your class from law school?

SARAH: Well, the causality in that statement seems a bit shaky to me. But who knows. I'd say it's my own little bit of *Lebenserfahrung*. That means "life experience" in German.

MARTIN: I see. And why couldn't you say "life experience"?

SARAH (smiling a bit): It looks so much more impressive in German, as a single word, starting with a capital letter.

MARTIN: I really thought she'd marry me.

SARAH (patiently, trying to explain): People are social constructions. When you're not Mayor any longer and when you're not in the position to pay for lavish hotel suites, you're simply not the same person you were before. Like seeing military men or policemen without their shiny uniforms. They're just people, and not half so impressive.

MARTIN: I can never think of uniforms without thinking of the doorman at the old Tyler City Chemicals. Your grandmother designed them. They were something. Nowadays the style is more relaxed, of course. No uniforms. No doorman, as far as I know.

SARAH: I had to go in last week on business. No doorman, just a woman at a desk.

MARTIN: You had business at Tyler City Chemicals?

SARAH: One of my clients works there.

MARTIN: I suppose that's not surprising. Tyler City Chemicals is still huge.

SARAH: They didn't even recognize my name. Kreuzinger, I mean.

MARTIN: So much has changed there.

SARAH: I wonder if you don't miss it, in a perverse way.

MARTIN: Just old times, perhaps. Youth. [Changing the subject back] Maybe your mother was right. I was infatuated with Becky.

SARAH: Most love starts with infatuation. It's only the next stage that decides what we ultimately call it. Like seeds. They all look the same when the fall from the tree. But some of them turn into little trees, and some of them don't.

MARTIN: The fallow ground and the rocky ground, and all that. I guess I was the rocky ground. [Pause.] Do you think Becky would take me back now? You've seen her.

SARAH: How can you even think of such a thing?

MARTIN: You don't have to be shocked.

SARAH: I'm not shocked, I'm appalled. Appalled that you're so desperate you would even think it possible.

MARTIN: So no?

SARAH: Of *course* she won't go back to you. You're a chapter in her life that's over. When was the last time you saw her?

MARTIN: Three years, or so. Just after my divorce from your mother became final.

SARAH: Did you ever ask her to marry you?

MARTIN: It was understood that we would marry. When the divorce came through, I asked her formally. I went out and bought a ring and everything. I got down on my knees, and I popped the question.

SARAH: And what did she say?

MARTIN: She cried, and said she knew she ought to marry me, since she was the cause of my divorce.

SARAH: I hope you didn't let her think she was the only reason.

MARTIN: I may have, just at first. But she knew it wasn't her.

SARAH: You see? She *is* bright. Think of how horrible it would have been if she'd married you. The two of you, living in a tiny apartment in Petersburg, you with some job where you could be anonymous and not merely the former Mayor of Tyler City, her with her secretary's job, or no job. Having to see each other day in and day out.

MARTIN: I never got that far in my thinking.

SARAH: She did you a favor by refusing.

MARTIN: Or maybe she was never as infatuated as I was.

SARAH: She acted as if she was, didn't she?

MARTIN: Yes. Of course, you're telling me that she was after the good times.

SARAH: You haven't been listening to a thing I've said. You *were* the good times. There is no "you" separable from what you did. Each person is his or her actions.

MARTIN: Did you learn that at Bryn Mawr?

SARAH: I learned it by living. The hard way. Oh, somebody has said something of the sort. Many somebodies. In fact, it's rather the fashion in intellectual circles. No ghost in the machine, as the soul is sometimes called.

MARTIN: No soul! How liberating. I think I like this philosophy. Does that mean we aren't responsible for our actions?

SARAH: If there's no "you" separate from your actions, how can you be responsible for them?

MARTIN: Doesn't that pose problems for the legal profession? Aren't you all the time trying to establish guilt or innocence?

SARAH: Just between you and me, yes. Which is why I've made a specialty of tax law. There's money in it, and you don't have to get involved in individuals. At least, not too much.

MARTIN: Aren't you being a bit too cold and analytical? A bit unforgiving of human foibles?

SARAH: Quite the opposite. Or rather, I don't forgive, because there is nothing to forgive. All human actions are as they are.

MARTIN (no longer really listening): I never earned as much money as you're earning. Poor Tommy. It really used to get to him that you were so smart. He felt stupid by comparison.

SARAH: He isn't, you know. But he has his own life now. He's accepted things. We all have to, right?

MARTIN: I suppose so. Yes. (Pause, changing the subject) Excuse the prying, but back in my day it was considered a father's duty to look out after the boys who were courting his daughter. I know all that's old hat, and I wouldn't presume to tell you what to do or who to see. But you're such an attractive girl. Are you seeing anybody?

SARAH: Are you sure you're not worrying about whether you're going to have any more grandchildren? Isn't Billy enough for you?

MARTIN: Hardly a grandchild in the usual sense. Biologically, of course. But not legitimate.

SARAH: An outdated concept, legitimacy. Indeed, the concept of parenthood is outdated. Or at least needs to be looked at more closely. Parenthood too should be understood as a concatenation of actions, and not merely a biological accident.

MARTIN: You mean that Sondra isn't a very good mother.

SARAH: I guess you can put it that way.

MARTIN: I suppose I'm old-fashioned enough that it bothers me they're not married. I mean, they live together, why shouldn't they get married?

Besides, I've only seen Billy three times. That's not a lot, given where Tommy lives.

SARAH: I thought you said it was better that way.

MARTIN: If he doesn't want to see me, I can't force him.

SARAH: You want to dandle your only grandchild on your knee, is that it?

MARTIN: Why not? If I'm going to be retired, how else am I to fill my time?

SARAH: Tommy doesn't want to be involved with you. You'll just have to accept that.

MARTIN (reflectively): Was it the indictment, I wonder, or Becky?

SARAH: Becky. Boys don't like to see their fathers fooling around with other women than their mothers. Especially not young ones. Freud had the slant on that one too. The father is supposed to bow out gracefully, sexually speaking. Not supposed to be too virile, in other words. To make room for the next generation.

MARTIN: But Tommy owes me so much. You don't know about what I did for him and that Tina.

SARAH: Tommy told me years ago. He resented it horribly.

MARTIN: Resented it? I saved his behind! He was sixteen and had knocked up a girl. Did he want to marry her?

SARAH: Probably not. And of course, I think you did the right thing. I mean, he went and did it again with Sondra, but at least by that time he was older. Old enough to sort of support her, out of school.

MARTIN: How can he resent me?

SARAH: He sees your getting Tina an abortion as an attempt to castrate him. Or some such thing. He was bound to resent you no matter what you did.

MARTIN: Castrate him!

SARAH: You know what he told me? He told me he asked you to adopt the child, and you refused.

MARTIN: He didn't ask me, at least not outright. I figured out that's where he was going.

SARAH: But you refused.

MARTIN: Of course I refused! I mean, what a can of worms! You don't mean to tell me he's angry with me because I didn't bring up his bastard as my son?

SARAH: And yet now he's bringing up another bastard, as you put it. Your only grandchild.

MARTIN: Is this a way of getting back at me for something I couldn't possibly have done? How would you like to have had a brother/nephew? Let's see, by now he'd be six, just ready to go into first grade. Would you have liked that? A little brother from your little brother?

SARAH: I just got through telling you that you shouldn't have done it. That's the rational situation. But the emotional situation is something else. And it's the emotional one that ultimately calls the tune.

MARTIN: What kind of a lawyer are you, daughter? I bet you're the strangest one in all of North Carolina. I mean, with convictions like that.

SARAH: Law is all clarity and light. Underneath, of course, is a world of twisting disorder. That world has its rules too. You can only learn them by living, not in school. Just the way you can follow a pattern made of squiggles and curves, but you can't describe it. For description to another person you have to stick to nice neat figures like circles and squares.

MARTIN: And are you going to give me a grandchild? One that I might be able to see every once in a while?

SARAH: Well, Dad, I'd say it's not likely.

MARTIN (considerably cast down): Aren't you interested in anyone?

SARAH: I thought you'd have guessed by now. I mean, where were the boyfriends? Did I ever talk to you about a man?

MARTIN (pause): I don't know that you did. Oh. I see how it is.

SARAH: I always did credit you with catching on quickly.

MARTIN: Well, I wasn't so quick on this one, was I? Or maybe I knew.

SARAH: Of course you knew.

MARTIN: In recent years we haven't talked a great deal at all. And when we did, it was all very intellectual. Like today.

SARAH: I'll talk personally now, if you like.

MARTIN: I don't know what to say.

SARAH: You could try being shocked, or outraged. Parents frequently are.

MARTIN: I thought we'd decided I quick on the uptake.

SARAH: So we did.

MARTIN: No outrage. Just a sense for myself of "that too?"

SARAH: Another in a list of your misfortunes, is that it?

MARTIN: I didn't mean it that way.

SARAH: I don't think anybody's life ends up the way they think they're going to. Or hardly anybody's. We can project patterns, but only in rare cases do we ever end up living our life according to them.

MARTIN: You sound like me, daughter.

SARAH: I am like you. That's why I'm sitting here with you today on this bench.

MARTIN: For which I'm grateful.

SARAH: I'm doing it because I want to. You're my father. [Pause.] Take me, for instance. I grew up like any other girl, thinking that I would marry a man and have children and live in a house with a picket fence. Of course, times being what they are, I assumed I'd have a job. That deal of the little woman doing all the cooking and cleaning while the man goes out and earns the living is dead, you know?

MARTIN: Just for the record, I don't think the women in our family have ever really been like that. We have a history of strong women.

SARAH: And weak men?

MARTIN (acknowledges the "touché" but goes on): We're supposed to be the decisive sex, but nobody gives us a manual explaining the world at birth. We have to plunge forward, but it's into darkness.

SARAH: I'm no man-hater, Dad. I'm not even sure I'm a feminist. All I really wanted was fairly traditional. A man with his job, me with my job, us with our kids. Only somewhere along the line I discovered that I didn't want to be married to a man. Or even, necessarily, sleep with one. I did, of course. You can do the things others expect for a time. Then you just give them up.

MARTIN (applying this to his own situation): I know.

SARAH: The problem is, the one I'm really interested in lives in Heidelberg.

MARTIN: You met her in your Fulbright year? That was three years ago.

SARAH: We write, we phone, that's where I go on vacation. Didn't you ever wonder why I went back to Germany?

MARTIN: I just thought you liked it. You know, nostalgia for a happy time.

SARAH: I was very happy there.

MARTIN: Why did you come back?

SARAH: I had to get on with my life. So did she.

MARTIN: What are you going to do about it?

SARAH: I can't give up my job and just move to Germany. I probably couldn't even get a work permit. Not being married to a German, that is.

MARTIN: What is this woman's name? Your friend's, I mean? Your—

SARAH: Lover? Ulrike. She's a writer.

MARTIN: What does she write?

SARAH: I should say, she wants to be a writer. She works in an ad agency and makes a lot of money.

MARTIN: Maybe she could come and live with you?

SARAH: I love her. She likes me. She won't do it. I know that too.

MARTIN (suddenly worried): You're not going to tell me you were interested in Becky, are you? I mean, that way?

SARAH (sincerely shocked): Dad! How revolting can you be? [Giggles.]

MARTIN: You know, I really think you're something of a prude.

SARAH: It was my girlhood as the Mayor's daughter. Still, it was a great girlhood, Dad. No regrets there.

[Sentimental pause.]

MARTIN: Tell me, my so-intelligent daughter. What of the millions of people who live lives like their parents, who are born and die in the same town, who live in houses with a picket fence? Do they have the same troubles making their lives turn out as you and I?

SARAH: I think it's a myth, boring people with predictable lives. Maybe some people, for some portion of their lives. But not most people, for most of their lives. Everybody is on the same roller-coaster. Only it's a roller-coaster without a track. It makes up its own trajectory as it goes along.

MARTIN: Do you think so?

SARAH: More and more. Our lives live us. We don't live them.

[Pause]

MARTIN: Do you hear the birds?

SARAH (ironic/sentimental): The sounds of new life.

MARTIN: When you're as old as I am, you'll appreciate them.

SARAH: I appreciate them now.

MARTIN (wistfully): You could force yourself, I suppose? To marry a man?

SARAH: Dad! Now you really are shocking me.

MARTIN (sheepishly, ashamed of himself): You have to love the other person, right?

SARAH: I love you.

MARTIN: I love you too.

SARAH: Shall we get up and walk in the spring?

MARTIN: Let's. [They stand.] Here, give me your arm. The smell of the earth. New life.

SARAH: The same old life. Just served up fresh.

MARTIN: Old wine in new bottles, eh? It tastes good every time. [They head offstage.]

Act Eleven

1982. SARAH and TOMMY. The living room of TOMMY's small house. Both brother and sister are sitting in chairs, each with a bottle of beer.

SARAH: Good beer.

TOMMY: Yeah, I like it.

SARAH: You drink too much of it.

TOMMY: What else am I supposed to do? Read books, like you? Remember, I'm not the brilliant one.

SARAH: But you *are* my little brother.

TOMMY: I'm a man now.

SARAH: You're still my little brother.

TOMMY: With a wife and kid.

SARAH: A common-law wife.

TOMMY: You want me to marry her?

SARAH: The last thing we want is a coke head in the family. I mean, any more than she already is in the family.

TOMMY: You smoked grass in college, I know you did. I heard Dad going on about it lots and lots. He was pissed at you for a while there. Though lately he's not, I guess.

SARAH (smiling a bit to herself): Dad and I have negotiated to find the area of our congruence.

TOMMY: I'm not in one of your law classes, you know.

SARAH: Come on, baby brother, buck up. So you don't have any construction work at the moment. You need to think in terms of something else. That's part of the reason I stopped by.

TOMMY: I notice you came when Sondra was out.

SARAH: You know I don't like Sondra. I don't like her habits, I don't like what she's doing to my nephew, I don't like her stringy blonde hair, I don't like the spaced-out way she talks. I don't even like her name.

TOMMY: That doesn't leave a lot, does it?

SARAH: Not a lot. Besides, she's upsetting mother.

TOMMY: Now I'm supposed to run my life so mom isn't upset? I've spent my whole life trying to please Dad, and be your little brother. In my own home I'm king. Get it?

SARAH: I get it. But you're not alone in this world, baby brother. You have a family.

TOMMY: Sometimes I think Sondra is lucky she doesn't have any family.

SARAH: No family that will talk to her, at any rate.

TOMMY: Better than that. They're all dead.

SARAH: Who'd bail you out financially if mother didn't?

TOMMY: It's not my fault if construction is slow.

SARAH: I doubt you've looked quite as hard as you might have. It's too easy to get a handout from Mom. And after all, since you have her only grandchild, it's easy, right?

TOMMY: Well, sis, you could go and produce a grandchild, couldn't you?

SARAH (withering): You know what I'm saying. You're not above mooching off her and using Billy for bait.

TOMMY: She loves Billy. She likes hearing about baby boxing.

SARAH: Entering an eight-year-old child in a boxing match is trashy.

TOMMY: It's fun. He likes it. It lets him get out his aggression. You should do the same thing. [He shadow-boxes at her to annoy her.]

SARAH: What's even more amazing to me is that there are lots of other fathers who want their sons to do the same thing. That's the idea, right? It's a league.

TOMMY (swig of beer): Yeah, a league. And it's fun. Fathers don't want their sons to grow up to be sissies, you know.

SARAH (sandpapery): Or fags, right?

TOMMY: (grinning at her: this is his hook on his sister): Right.

SARAH: Okay, baby brother. Listen up. I'm telling you that the freeloading has got to stop. Go get a job.

TOMMY: You sound just like Dad. Or the way Dad would if he still talked to me.

SARAH: You're the one who doesn't talk to him.
TOMMY: Same difference.
SARAH: I think you should make things up with him.
TOMMY: Why?
SARAH: It's important to get along with your parents.
TOMMY: I swear, I used to think you were the wild one. You know, the rebel. You're more like them than they are. I'm the outlaw.
SARAH: No one is an outlaw in this family.
TOMMY: People who go to places like Bryn Mawr don't get lost in the cracks.
SARAH: Is that how you see yourself? Lost in the cracks?
TOMMY (sullenly): Something like that.
SARAH: You're just coasting.
TOMMY: What am I supposed to do? No work, my father can't show his face in Tyler City, my mother watches the shopping channel on the television all day. My wife is a coke head . . . What do you want?
SARAH: I just want to drink my beer.
TOMMY: Fine by me.
SARAH [ignores him, takes a swig, sits back]: You've done more work on the house since I was here.
TOMMY: Gotta put all that construction experience to work, ya know.
SARAH: You've developed quite a sense of humor. Used to be you were the quiet type.
TOMMY: Yeah? Well, maybe that was because you were talking all the time and didn't listen to me. None of you.
SARAH: Now I want to talk to you about Sondra. I know a sister probably shouldn't try to talk to a man [she emphasizes the words "a man" for sarcastic effect] about his common-law wife.
TOMMY: That's right. It's a thankless job. Which means I won't thank you, right?
SARAH: I've never understood what it is you see in Sondra.
TOMMY: She's nice to me.
SARAH: When she's not flying high. [Suddenly suspicious] You'd better not be doing that junk too. It's poison.
TOMMY: Lay off.
SARAH (apparently convinced): Okay. [Re-groups.] All right. So she's nice to you. That's nice. But think of the way she's raising Billy.

TOMMY: Nothin' wrong with the way she's raising Billy. Besides, I'm raising Billy too.

SARAH: Yes, to box. And to mooch off of mother.

TOMMY (sullenly): Nothin' wrong with boxing.

SARAH: Tommy, I don't know if I can get through to you on this.

TOMMY: So why don't you save your breath?

SARAH: Because it's too important. And because I don't see you that often.

TOMMY: Nothin' wrong with Billy.

SARAH: Billy is a perfectly nice little boy, and potentially a normal member of society.

TOMMY: Potentially? You mean he's not normal? Take my word for it. He's normal. You're the one who's not normal.

SARAH (ignoring this): He's got a short attention span. He may be hyperactive. Don't you see that?

TOMMY: He's not going to be henpecked by a pack of women like I was.

SARAH (shrill despite herself): Henpecked?

TOMMY: When it wasn't Mom it was you. Both of you first-class yakkers.

SARAH (not getting the better of this exchange): I'm trying to identify this situation as a problem. You're out of work, Sondra spends all her time high on coke, you get hand-outs from mother—

TOMMY: And that's another thing. If Mom feels like she wants to give some money to her only grandchild, I'm not gonna be the one to say she can't. And neither are you.

SARAH: She's giving money to Sondra for groceries, and Sondra is spending it on drugs.

TOMMY: That's a lie.

SARAH: Ask mother. Last month she gave Sondra $200 for food, and two days later Sondra came back and said she's lost it, so mother gave her another $200. And then the next day you come by with Billy and say you've had to go out and get some fast food for him because there's nothing in the house. It's happened again and again.

TOMMY (sullenly): I don't believe you.

SARAH (reasoning): Don't bother asking Sondra. She'll deny it anyway.

TOMMY: Of course she'll deny it. It isn't true.

SARAH: Where is Sondra getting the money for the drugs, according to you?

TOMMY: I dunno. She has friends. Some of them give it to her.

SARAH: The money or the coke? I don't believe either one.

TOMMY: She works sometimes. She helps out down at the dump. She's the receptionist.

SARAH: I bet they're the ones who get her the coke. But nobody gives that stuff away. Why would they give it to her when they can sell it and make a fortune?

TOMMY: She's got friends.

SARAH: The only reason I'm not going to the police is that she hasn't done anything dangerous with Billy. Yet.

TOMMY: She's a good mother.

SARAH: Goldfish are better mothers than she is. And goldfish eat their babies.

TOMMY: She leaves him here with me. I'm here a lot. I watch TV.

SARAH: Sure she leaves him with you. She can't take him where she goes.

TOMMY (shrewdly, thinking): Well, then I can't get a job if I have to look after Billy, can I?

SARAH (pause): You win, slugger.

TOMMY (pleased with himself): For once.

SARAH (trying again): Tommy, do you have any idea why I was so upset? I mean, can you tell me, in your own words, why I might have come to see you today?

TOMMY: Yeah, sure. You're jealous of my family and jealous of my link to Mom.

SARAH (hurt): I'm sorry you think my motives are so low.

TOMMY: All right, you tell me why you came by.

SARAH: That's what I've been trying to do.

TOMMY: Yeah, but you were yelling. Try it again and don't yell and I may listen better.

SARAH: The situation is frustrating for me, Tommy.

TOMMY: You think I like it?

SARAH (the good pedagogue, seeing her chance): What do you dislike?

TOMMY: What do I dislike? Jeesh, do you gotta ask? I mean, I spend all day sitting on my behind looking after a kid, my wife's out, all I do is watch television and go visit Mom.

SARAH: I know it's bothering you. You're even starting to get a beer gut.

TOMMY: I don't get out. Construction, it keeps you healthy at any rate.

SARAH: Tommy, do you get to see the fellows very much?

TOMMY: Nah. Once they came here, but Sondra came home and raised hell. So I see them once in a while.

SARAH: When you're not baby-sitting, right?

TOMMY: Sure. What do you think? I'd take the kid to a poker game?

SARAH: You grew up in a different kind of household than Sondra did. You take different kinds of things for granted. One of the things you take for granted is that the wife will make an effort to take care of the children. So the husband can have an occasional night out.

TOMMY (slipping out of the trap): Just like Susie Homemaker, huh?

SARAH (through clenched teeth): Well, not exactly. Of course, some realignment of the paradigm is necessary to compensate for structural differences between the time of its inception and the present.

TOMMY: I knew if I got you upset enough you'd turn back into the professor. It's not the wife that's the problem, not the mother. It's the sister.

SARAH: This is only the second time I've come to your house.

TOMMY: Because you don't like Sondra.

SARAH: My point is that I'm not trying to run your life.

TOMMY: It sounds like it to me.

SARAH: Think of Billy!

TOMMY: What do you want me to think about Billy? I'm not going to dump Sondra, and Billy is her son. What if she takes him away from me? Where will I be then? I love him. I love Billy.

SARAH: My point is exactly that you have to think of him. And as for taking him, there are ways to make sure that Sondra doesn't take him. In fact, there are ways to get her out of the picture entirely. If you'd only let me do a little investigation, I think we could get good grounds.

TOMMY: For what?

SARAH: For having her declared an unfit mother, for starters.

TOMMY: She's the only mother Billy knows. What are you trying to do to him?

SARAH: She's a menace. She's dangerous to Billy, and she's stealing from your mother.

TOMMY: She loves Billy. And you're jealous.

SARAH: I'm jealous of your broken-down house and your construction jobs when you can get them and of your television daytime soap operas and of your coke-head thieving wife. I'm jealous of all that, right?

TOMMY (giving in): Maybe not.

SARAH: All right.

TOMMY: So what are you if you're not jealous?

SARAH: First, I am sad for you. Second, I am mad for mother. Third, I am concerned for Billy. Is that clear enough?

TOMMY: I guess so.

SARAH (relaxing a bit in victory): I knew you would be hard to convince, but I had no idea how hard. I mean, in a way it's good that you don't have the same opinion about Sondra that everybody else does. That would be too spooky, if you saw her clearly and still stayed with her. Let's just say you're blinded by love.

TOMMY: Blinded by love. I like that. It sounds like a song.

SARAH: I bet it is, somewhere.

TOMMY: Maybe I could write it. I've always wanted to write songs. You think I could do that rather than construction?

SARAH: I hardly think—

TOMMY: Hey, sis, you told me to get a job, didn't you?

SARAH (seeing that he is kidding): Okay, sure. Write it. I hope you make a million bucks. Then I can quit my job and you can support us all.

TOMMY: You'll never quit your job. You like being a law professor. Telling people what to do. It's what you were born for.

SARAH (suddenly vulnerable): You don't think I'm bossy, do you? I mean, you know I have your best interests at heart?

TOMMY (relenting): I know you do, sis. [Pause.] Hey sis, how is Mom?

SARAH: What do you mean, how is Mom? You see her more often than I do.

TOMMY: Yeah, I know. I see her. But I don't really spend all that much time there. I go in, she's got the television on to the shopping channel, with the police band radio blaring away. Most times she's got a drink in her hand. You think I'm bad. With me it's only beer. I drop the kid, she gives me some money, and later on I come back and get him.

SARAH: Then you know how Mom is. She drinks too much, and she does nothing but sit at the kitchen table and watch television. If I didn't have Mrs. Cropp come in to fix her food every other day, I think she'd live off of Chinese food and pizzas. Delivered. I arranged for the lawn service, so she doesn't even have to water the lawn. The only time she goes out is to get the mail. Though it's all ads.

TOMMY: Is it really that bad?

SARAH: She never got over Dad.

TOMMY: Does he ever call or anything?

SARAH: She wouldn't talk to him.

TOMMY: Do you think he still loves her? I mean, just a little?

SARAH: Who knows? I know he misses our life before. I don't think he really liked politics. That was part of the problem.

TOMMY: He didn't like being mayor? You coulda fooled me.

SARAH: Yeah. He fooled everybody. Including himself, for a while.

TOMMY: What do you think he really wanted to be?

SARAH: I don't think he ever found out.

TOMMY: So what does he do with his time?

SARAH: Oh, I think he watches TV too, and takes walks. And drinks, like mother.

TOMMY: Geesh, and you object to Sondra's using a little coke.

SARAH: It seems strange to think of them as old.

TOMMY: They are. They're old.

SARAH: They were young once too, you know, and full of dreams.

TOMMY: Are we young and full of dreams?

SARAH: I know I'm not, at any rate. A bit short in the dream department, one might say.

TOMMY: I'm sorry for Mom. I mean, I like her. I love her.

SARAH: I love them both. I love us all. Mother, Father, Daughter, Son. I love our past. Or maybe it's just my vision of our past. For one brief moment, you know, it was perfect. Father mayor. Mother faithful helpmeet. Daughter Bryn Mawr-bound. Son Slugger of Coolidge High.

TOMMY (his flash of perception): Well, if it changed maybe that means it wasn't all that perfect to begin with. Like planets that come into a pattern for just a second and then go out.

SARAH: You may have something there, baby brother. Next time, why don't you spend a little more time at Mom's? I mean, don't just drop off Billy. Stay a few minutes before you pocket your handout.

TOMMY: Sis—

SARAH: Okay. I won't say any more. But one day Sondra is going to do something really major. I hope she doesn't do it with Billy around.

TOMMY: She wouldn't do anything to hurt Billy. She loves Billy. Anyway, she can't have an accident or anything, because she doesn't drive. She hitches rides with friends.

SARAH: Tommy, you can't trust coke-heads.

TOMMY: But she's my wife. Well, sort of.

SARAH: Yes, and she's unstable. Sort of. One day you're going to have Billy alone, Tommy. I just want to warn you.

TOMMY: I practically have him alone now. If it wasn't for Mom I don't know where I'd be.

SARAH: On second thought, maybe we shouldn't worry about another job right now.

TOMMY: I knew you'd come around. It isn't like I don't want to work. Want another beer?

SARAH: One's enough for me.

TOMMY: If we're done talking, want to watch some baseball?

SARAH (looking at her watch): If you tell me who's good and who's not. Ten minutes. Then I have to go. I have some papers to correct.

TOMMY: Okay, it's a deal. [Fiddles with dials.] Look. Here's the Orioles. Playing New York. Piece of cake. [Pause.] Here's Walker, he's coming up now. Let me tell you about Walker. He had a lot of promise but recently he's been flubbing up something awful . . . [The voice ends in mid-phrase.]

ACT TWELVE

1989. SARAH and BARBARA. The library of the old house, the one that BARBARA moved to as a teenager. BARBARA is in an armchair, watching television. The door to the next room is ajar. It is evening. The sound is low enough that the scene can be played with the television running, but the set is turned to the audience so that the images are visible. BARBARA has a drink at her hand, which she sips occasionally. Then, finally, SARAH's voice calling faintly: It's me! Hello!

BARBARA (as if having to tear her eyes away from the set, or not looking away at all): In here! [Her voice is somewhat gravelly with age and too much drinking.]

SARAH (comes in. She is older, well-dressed, obviously successful. She stoops and kisses her mother on the forehead.): Hello, mother.

BARBARA (looks up briefly from the television): Hello dear.

SARAH: How are you, mother?

BARBARA (seeming to accept the inevitability of carrying on this conversation with her daughter and turning away resolutely from the television): I'm all right.

SARAH (hovering over her for a moment): I didn't know how you'd be feeling.

BARBARA: I'm fine. I'm feeling fine.

SARAH: You didn't sound quite so fine when I called earlier, so I thought I should come see you myself. I was sorry to have to tell you over the telephone, but I thought you should know, and I couldn't come until now.

BARBARA: It's all right, Sarah. Your father is nothing to me now. His dying doesn't change anything.

SARAH (a bit flustered at her mother's reaction, and sitting in a chair nearby): I thought maybe it would be better for you not to be alone, today. So I came.

BARBARA: I made peace with that years ago. You just have to let it go. That way it can't hurt you any longer.

SARAH (encouraging her to talk about it, suspecting that she is not so blasé as she appears): I know that you were really hurt by Dad leaving. Back then.

BARBARA: Yes.

SARAH: I wonder what made Dad do it.

BARBARA (matter-of-factly): He was in love with that girl. What was her name?

SARAH: Becky.

BARBARA: All that seems a long time ago.

SARAH (looking around): I'm glad you decided to move back into the old house. Grandmother Nadine would be happy to think you were here.

BARBARA: I didn't really grow up in it. It was built when I was already in my teens. When Tyler City Chemicals took off.

SARAH (encouraging her to talk): That's right.

BARBARA: It's funny, your grandmother and I got closer in her last years than we had ever been before.

SARAH (encouraging): Why was that?

BARBARA: I had been so close to Daddy, and he always held a grudge against her for forcing him into chemicals. Even though it turned out to be a gold mine. I mean, she was right. So now I thought, why not? It's difficult to take one parent's point of view over the other when one of them is dead and the other doddering.

SARAH: Sort of the way we've made up too.

BARBARA: I guess I'm the doddering one, then. Seeing as how I'm not dead.

SARAH: Sorry. Didn't mean that. [Pause, looks around.] I remember coming to visit here as a child.

BARBARA: Do you? After a while it was too painful for your father, him having left Tyler City and all.

SARAH: It was some house back then. Servants, maids, a butler.

BARBARA: Mother always had trouble keeping cooks. She was so controlling. Of me too.

SARAH: You weren't controlling of me. I came to appreciate that later.

BARBARA: I'm glad. It's always such a temptation to try to get children to do things your way. They never do. When a baby comes out from between your legs you feel you've created it. It's odd to have to accept that really, it's an alien thing that's grown inside you.

SARAH (trying to be light): Sounds like a sci-fi thriller.

BARBARA: Assume complete difference from the parents, that's my advice to whomever wants it, and be pleasantly surprised by any similarities. You and Tommy certainly couldn't be more dissimilar.

SARAH: From each other, or from you and Daddy?

BARBARA: From anybody. Sometimes I really think families aren't what they're cracked up to be.

SARAH: Family is very important to me.

BARBARA: Not to me. People who go on about blood being thicker than water don't know what they're talking about. Blood is the thinnest substance there is.

SARAH: I was right to come by.

BARBARA: I'm always glad to see you. My brilliant daughter.

SARAH: I get it all from you, mother. Who says blood means nothing?

BARBARA: It's true. I was all right in my day. So was Grandmother Nadine. The women in our family have always been bright. But back then, we were supposed to help our husbands. I tried. For that matter, Grandmother Nadine tried. She was a real firecracker. [Gets a thought] Do you know, shortly before she died she explained to me with great solemnity that my brother, the one who died in the war—

SARAH (interrupting, to show she is following): Uncle Martin?

BARBARA: Uncle Martin, whom I loved so dearly . . . that he wasn't your grandfather's child after all. I still don't know whether to believe her or not. I mean, she was a little weak in the head by that point, but why would she make it up? She claimed she'd had an affair with Dad's business partner, Jim Masterson.

SARAH: Bill Masterson's father?

BARBARA: I was supposed to marry Bill Masterson, you know. It doesn't matter now. I mean the story about Martin. True, not true—no one will ever be sure.

SARAH: You're not upset your mother might have been unfaithful to your father?

BARBARA: Things like that matter only to the young.

SARAH (doesn't know how to respond; changes the subject by gesturing around her at the house): It all comes back to Tyler City Chemicals, doesn't it? I know you're proud that Grandfather started it. Despite all the problems it's brought us.

BARBARA: I suppose I am, in a way. It always gave me the feeling of being important. Barbara Rush Kreuzinger, of Tyler City Chemicals.

SARAH: These last few years have been wild ones for everybody. Boom years.

BARBARA: I don't know much about economics, but I do know that booms tend to be followed by busts. [Changing the subject] I worry less about Tommy nowadays.

SARAH: It helps to have Sondra out of the picture.

BARBARA: It got to the point where she took money out of my handbag and then lied about it. Did I ever tell you that?

SARAH: You've forgotten the whole long discussion we had about what to do?

BARBARA: Did we have a discussion?

SARAH: You shouldn't drink so much, mother.

BARBARA: What else am I supposed to do with my time?

SARAH: Get out. Do things. More than just to pick up the mail.

BARBARA (ignoring this): What ever happened to her?

SARAH: To who? Or I should say, to whom?

BARBARA: Sondra. Now you're not paying attention.

SARAH: After we got the court order forbidding her to come near Tommy and Billy, she left town. I think she went back to Richmond.

BARBARA: Well, good riddance.

SARAH: Tommy's doing better since he started working again.

BARBARA: His life isn't going to be the easiest. Now he's got work, tomorrow he may not have. I used to worry about him, living from job to job. It was never our way. We knew where the money was coming from. And even if he's not quite as bright as you, dear, he could have found more steady employment.

SARAH: I think he likes the change.

BARBARA: I hope so. Of course, your father's . . . thing hit him hard. And he was so young at the time. I've often thought there was a connection between the way he began to drift and that business.

SARAH: Of course there was, mother. It's the one thing I find hard to forgive Father.

BARBARA: You must forgive him, dear. We must forgive everyone.

SARAH: I know that, in theory.

BARBARA: Baseball is more suitable for Billy that that boxing nonsense. Tommy would bring me pictures of the boy with gloves on that were bigger than he was.

SARAH: He may turn out all right after all.

BARBARA: They come to see me maybe twice, three times a week now. And not just for money.

SARAH: That *is* a change.

BARBARA: I used to hope, after Sondra left, that you would take Billy. Or that you and Tommy would move in together. I mean, since you'll never marry, and as far as I know have no commitments—

SARAH (brusquely): No, I have no commitments.

BARBARA (apologetic): I'm so sorry it didn't work out with your friend from Germany. I know you'd hoped it would.

SARAH: She made other plans.

BARBARA: Couldn't you have found someone else yourself? I mean, with men and women, that's the way these things go.

SARAH: Who was your someone else? I loved Ulrike. In some ways, I still do. It's not so easy getting over someone you've really loved.

BARBARA: I know.

SARAH: I did think of it. Helping raise Tommy, I mean.

BARBARA: Your values are so . . . how shall I say . . . so solid.

SARAH: You mean I'm a dyed-in-the-wool conservative. It's true. Tailored suits and early to bed. You couldn't have gotten yourself a more stodgy daughter, in some ways.

BARBARA: It's because you had your rebellion when you were young. It always happens that way.

SARAH: I know that's your theory. It may be right.

BARBARA: What did Tommy say?

SARAH: He wanted to have Billy all to himself. He said he loved every one of his fingers and toes and he wasn't going to share him with anybody. And he went right on taking him to boxing, and now baseball and who knows what else.

BARBARA: It's a shame. I mean, you could have exposed him to art, and music, and philosophy. The finer things of life.

SARAH: I'll get in my licks soon enough. Besides, as you say, kids sometimes turn out the opposite of what their parents want. Tommy may think he's raising another construction worker jock, but in fact he may find himself with a math genius or something. Billy's very quick, you know.

BARBARA: He always did strike me as a bright little boy.

SARAH: I decided I didn't want to raise Billy. Not just because Tommy didn't want me to. I mean, talk about gestures of renunciation, that would have been one. "Frustrated Old Maid Who Prefers Women Devotes Herself To Raising Brother's Only Son." I may not have gotten it on with Ulrike, but that doesn't mean I have to become a living symbol of being co-opted by the patriarchal society.

BARBARA: I'm not quite sure I'm following you.

SARAH: It doesn't matter. Did you know Tommy wanted you and Dad to raise his son? The one that was aborted? Or didn't you ever hear about that?

BARBARA: Aborted? Oh dear. I don't think I want to hear about this. I didn't hear then and there's no point now. I barely have what it takes to watch the soaps. Once, I remember, I would have looked down on it as so much nonsense. Not that there was television in my youth, not like there is now. Howdy Doody, that was television that I remember. Now look at it.

SARAH: You do all right, mother.

BARBARA: All right for an old lady with a house that's too big for her and too full of memories.

SARAH: You were the one who wanted to live in it. The house, I mean.

BARBARA: It seemed fitting. [Suddenly] I hope you'll live in this house some day. You should, you know. When I'm gone.

SARAH: You're just melancholy today.

BARBARA (heedless, going on): I don't think I'll last much longer than your father did, my dear. And besides, you're the right person to live here. So reliable. The only one in the family who could do justice to the old place. Me, I live in it with most of the rooms just gathering dust. And old houses like this aren't the fashion nowadays.

SARAH: Let's not talk about that now.

BARBARA: I'm leaving it to you in my will, at any rate. You'll have to make the decision.

SARAH: All right, mother, if it makes you happy.

BARBARA (abruptly): He was the love of my life, you know.

SARAH: Daddy?

BARBARA: Funny that you still call him that, and you a middle-aged woman. Yes. Your father.

SARAH: You *are* sad. I knew it.

BARBARA: I close my eyes and see him visiting me here in this house, full of life and youth. So was I back then, though it's difficult to imagine now. I can see his handsome face, see his hands that made me shiver when they touched me.

SARAH (wanting to ward off this intimacy): Mother—

BARBARA (talking almost to herself): Feel his lips when they kissed me.

SARAH says nothing, looking away.

BARBARA: I would have died for him. And when he left me I cursed him for months. For years. [Pause.] He hurt me so.

SARAH (somewhat lamely): I don't think he meant to.

BARBARA: I wonder if he loved me. I mean, in the last years. You'd think that a love like ours would never die, no matter what the people did in their actions.

SARAH: I'm sure he did, mother.

BARBARA: After his girlfriend refused to marry him, he led a rather sorry existence. Always trying to get away from his past. Like me, I suppose. [Lifts the glass and sips.] And to think he would have been Governor Kreuzinger.

SARAH: No use crying over that one, mother.

BARBARA: Maybe I was working so hard to make it happen I didn't see what was happening with him.

SARAH: You'd have liked to be the Governor's wife, wouldn't you?

BARBARA: I can't deny it. Not just me either. One day your grandmother went on a tour of the Governor's mansion just so she would know how to redecorate when we moved in.

SARAH: She must have been disappointed.

BARBARA: As much as I was, if not more. Just goes to show you, you can only push people so far.

SARAH: But you weren't pushing him, were you?

BARBARA: Some people are self-destructive. Your father may have been one of them. If so, he got what he wanted. You said he was found dead in his apartment?

SARAH: A neighbor who checked on him didn't get an answer and finally called the police. Apparently he had a heart attack. Of course, all the drinking hadn't helped. Or the loneliness.

BARBARA: Poor Martin.

[Phone rings.]

BARBARA: Hello? [Pause.] Oh yes, Tommy. How nice of you to call. [Pause.] Yes, Sarah's here. Do you want to talk to her? [Pause.] She tried to get you earlier, but you were out. [Pause.] Yes, I know you were at work. I think it's wonderful. [Pause.] Sarah and I are just sitting here talking about old times. My old times, really. And the future too. [Pause.] No, not my future, Billy's. [Pause.] Give him my love. [Pause.] You don't have to come over. You can just come tomorrow, the way we said. [Pause.] Don't be silly. From 11 to 5, that's fine. [Pause.] I know you loved him. [Pause.] Come a little early, and we'll talk. [Pause.] All right, I'll talk and you can listen. [Pause.] Give him a kiss from me, and tell him his Grandmother loves him. [Pause.] All right. [Pause.] Yes, thank you. Good-bye. [Hangs up.] [To SARAH] Not the most articulate of boys, that Tommy.

SARAH: No, but a good boy. As you would say.

BARBARA: I think he turned out all right. Better than I thought he would.

SARAH (suddenly feeling she has to say something to sum it all up): Mother, I'm so sorry. I mean, for it all.

BARBARA: For what? You can't take on the responsibility for the world, you know. You used to say that people were their situations, do you remember?

SARAH: I've changed my mind.

BARBARA: I knew you would.

SARAH: There's something inside of us that wants to reflect on things. Worry about them. Regrets that we didn't do better, and wonders why.

BARBARA: Usually called the conscience.

SARAH: I didn't used to believe in things like that. Now I do. It seems odd that one would go through so many years of schooling and life only to go back to a notion one learned in childhood.

BARBARA: There is some advantage to listening to your mother, you know.

SARAH: You're right. I should listen to my mother. [Smiles at her, then] I'd like to stay, but I have work to do.

BARBARA: You always were responsible. Go. I appreciate the time you've spent with me.

SARAH: I feel bad I can't come more often.

BARBARA: I know you're thinking about me. Phone every once in a while, will you?

SARAH: Of course. [Gently.] Good-bye, mother. [She goes to the door, turns around and gives her mother a last rather wan smile. Silence, except for the television.]

BARBARA (suddenly yelling to her, though Sarah is undoubtedly too far away to hear; the words are spaced out and the tone is angry): Don't pity me! [The cry reverberates; in a moment there is the faint sound of a car starting and leaving. BARBARA stares into the air for a moment or two, then slowly, her head turns back to the television.]

Notes

Shklovsky, "Art as Technique," page 22.
I considered this connection in *Modernism and its Discontents*, Chapter Three.
Gertrude Stein, "Composition as Explanation." T. S. Eliot, "Tradition and the Individual Talent." Robert Hughes, *The Shock of the New*, pages 188-89.
Virginia Woolf, *Jacob's Room* and *The Waves*.
I've considered this in an essay called "On Technique: The Church Exhibition."
As developed by A. J. Greimas in works such as *Sémiotique et sciences sociales* (Paris: Seuil, 1976).
Langer, page 18.

Bibliography

Abrams, M. H. *The Mirror and the Lamp: Romantic Theory and the Critical Tradition*. Boston: Norton, 1958.

Barthes, Roland. *S/Z: An Essay*. Translated by Richard Miller. Preface by Richard Howard. New York: Hill and Wang, 1975.

Eliot, T.S. "Tradition and the Individual Talent." In *Selected Prose of T.S. Eliot*, 37-44. Edited and with an introduction by Frank Kermode. New York: Harvest, 1975.

Hughes, Robert. *The Shock of the New*. New York: Knopf, 1980.

Fleming, Bruce. "The Autobiography of Gertrude Stein." In *Prize Stories 1990: The O. Henry Awards*, 352-370. New York: Doubleday, 1990.

---*An Essay in Post-Romantic Literary Theory: Art, Artifact and the Innocent Eye*. Lewiston, NY: Mellen, 1990.

---*Modernism and its Discontents: Philosophical Problems of Twentieth-Century Literary Theory*. New York: Peter Lang, 1992.

---"A Student's Guide to the Classics." *Antioch Review* 61.3 (2003): 477-497.

---"On Technique in Painting: The Church Exhibition." *Centennial Review* 40.1 (1996): 159-169.

Langer, Suzanne K. *Philosophy in a New Key: A Study in the*

Symbolism of Reason, Rite and Art. Cambridge, MA: Harvard University Press, 1957.

O'Neill, Eugene. *Long Day's Journey into Night.* New Haven: Yale University Press, 1962.

---*Strange Interlude.* In *Nine Plays,* 485-686. New York: Modern Library, 1941.

Perkins, David, ed. *English Romantic Writers.* New York: Harcourt, Brace, and World, 1967.

Shklovsky, Victor. "Art as Technique." In *Russian Formalist Criticism: Four Essays*, 3-24. Lincoln, NE: University of Nebraska Press, 1965.

Stein, Gertrude. "Composition as Explanation." In *Selected Writings of Gertrude Stein*, 511-524. Edited by Carl Van Vechten. New York: Vintage, 1962.

Welleck, René and Austin Warren. *Theory of Literature.* New York: Harvest, 1956.

Wilson, Edmund. *Axel's Castle: A Study of the Imaginative Literature of 1870-1930.* New York: Scribner's, 1953.

Woolf, Virginia. *Jacob's Room.* New York: Harvest, 1950.

---*The Waves.* New York: Harvest, 1950.

Index

Abrams, M. H.
   Mirror and the Lamp, The, viii
Abstract Expressionism, xiiv
ambiguity
   New Criticism, xiv
Aristotle, ix
"Autobiography of Gertrude Stein, The"
   Fleming, Bruce, xvii
Axel's Castle
   Wilson, Edmund, xii
Bach, J. S., viii
Barthes, Roland
   S/Z, xv
Baudelaire, Charles
   "Albatross, L'," viii
Beatles, The, x
Beuys, xiii
Braque, Georges, xiii
Broadway music, xii
collage, xiii
"Composition as Explanation"
   Stein, Gertrude, xi
Corbusier, Le, xii
   Radiant City, xii
de Kooning, Willem, xii
deconstructionism, xv
"Defense of Poetry"
   Shelley, Percy, vix
Derrida, Jacques, xv
Duchamp, Marcel
   ready-mades, xiii
earthworks
   Smithson, James, xviii
Eliot, T. S.
   "Tradition and the Individual Talent," xi
   "Waste Land, The," xiii
England, vi

"Erased de Kooning Drawing"
   Rauschenberg, Robert, xiii
Essay in Post-Romantic Theory, An
   Fleming, Bruce, xvii
"extrinsic" criticism
   Welleck, René, and Austin Warren, vix
Fleming, Bruce
   "Autobiography of Gertrude Stein, The," xvii
   Essay in Post-Romantic Literary Theory, An, xvii
   Modernism and its Discontents: Philosophical Problems of Twentieth-Century Literary Theory, viii
   "Student's Guide to the Classics, A," xvii
Foucault, Michel, viii, xvi
Freud, Sigmund, x
Geary, Frank, xii
Gris, Juan, xiii
Guggenheim Museum, xii, xiii
Hirshhorn Museum, xiii
Hughes, Robert
   Shock of the New, The, xi
Hugo, Victor
   "Mages, Les," viii
Iceman Comet, The
   O'Neill, Eugene, xxi
Industrial Revolution, vix
irony
   New Criticism, xiv
Johns, Jasper, xii
Joyce, James
   Finnegans Wake, xii
Lamartine, Alphonse de, xix
Langer, Suzanne
   Philosophy in a New Key, v, xvi

Lévi-Strauss, Claude
  semiotic squares, xv
Liszt, Franz
  Les Preludes, xix
Long Day's Journey into Night
  O'Neill, Eugene, xvii
Mahler, Gustave, xx
Marx, Karl, x
Medieval Age, vi
Mendelssohn, Felix, xi
Mirror and the Lamp, The
  Abrams, M. H., viii
Modernism, x, xii
Modernism and its Discontents: Philosophical Problems of Twentieth-Century Literary Theory
  Fleming, Bruce, viii
Mourning Becomes Electra
  O'Neill, Eugene, xx
New Criticism, xiiii
novel (birth), vi
O'Neill, Eugene
  Iceman Cometh, The, xxi
  Long Day's Journey into Night, xviii
  Mourning Becomes Electra, xx
  Strange Interlude, xv
Philadelphia Museum of Art, xiii
philistines, ix
Philosophy in a New Key
  Langer, Suzanne, v
  Picasso, Pablo, xiii
post-Modernism, xii
Pound, Ezra, xiii
Preludes, Les
  Liszt, Franz, xix
Presley, Elvis, x
Prince, Richard, xiii
Radiant City
  Corbusier, Le, xi
Rauschenberg, Robert
  Erased de Kooning drawing, xiii
Renaissance, vi
Romanticism, v, vii, viii, ix
  literary theory, xvii
Russian Formalists, xi
S/Z
  Barthes, Roland, xv
Shakespeare, William
  soliliquy, xxii
Shelley, Percy
  "Defense of Poetry," ix, xvi
Shkloveky, Victor
  "Art as Technique," x
Smithson, James
  earthworks, xviii
Southeast Asian drama, xviii
Speer, Albert, xiii
Stein, Gertrude
  "Composition as Explanation," xi
  essays, xii
Strange Interlude
  O'Neill, Eugene, xvii
structuralism, xv
"A Student's Guide to the Classics"
  Fleming, Bruce, xvii
Sydney opera house, xiii
symbolic thought (Langer), v
"Tradition and the Individual Talent"
  Eliot, T. S., xi
Victorian era, x
Vienna, xi
Villiers de l'Isle Adam
  Axel (character), xii
Wagner, Richard, xxii
Warhol, Andy, xii
Welleck, xv
Welleck, René and Austin Warren
  "extrinsic" criticism, ix
Wilson, Edmund
  Axel's Castle, xii
Woolf, Virginia, x
  Jacob's Room, xii
  Waves, The, xii

About the Author

Bruce Fleming won an O. Henry Award for his first published story, "The Autobiography of Gertrude Stein" (1989) and in 2005, the Antioch Review Award for Distinguished Prose, a career award. His experimental novel *Twilley* (1997) was compared by critics to works by Henry James, T.S. Eliot, Proust, Thoreau, and David Lynch. He has published a book of dance essays, *Sex, Art and Audience* (2000); a memoir *Journey to the Middle of the Forest* (2008); many scholarly and literary-theoretical books; and articles and essays in literary quarterlies and publications such as the *Village Voice*, *The Washington Post*, and *The Nation*. His series of philosophical books includes *Art and Argument: What Words Can't Do and What They Can* (2003), *Sexual Ethics* (2004), and *Science and the Self* (2004) and *Disappointment, or The Light of Common Day* (2006). These culminated in *The New Tractatus: Summing Up Everything* (2007). Other books include *Life, Death and Literature at the U.S. Naval Academy* (2005) and *Why Liberals and Conservatives Clash* (2006). His academic degrees, from Haverford College, The University of Chicago, and Vanderbilt University, are in philosophy and comparative literature. He is an English professor at the U.S. Naval Academy, Annapolis, where he has taught literature for more than twenty years.

www.ingramcontent.com/pod-product-compliance
Lightning Source LLC
Chambersburg PA
CBHW030117010526
44116CB00005B/283